T0294712

# THE
# SUMMONS
# OF THE
# LORD OF
# HOSTS

# THE
# SUMMONS
# OF THE
# LORD OF
# HOSTS

*Tablets of Bahá'u'lláh*

*Bahá'í*
PUBLISHING

Wilmette, Illinois

Bahá'í Publishing, 401 Greenleaf Avenue,
Wilmette, Illinois 60091-2844

18  17  16  15     4  3  2  1

**Library of Congress Cataloging-in-Publication Data**
Bahá'u'lláh, 1817–1892.
    [Correspondence. Selections. English]
    The summons of the Lord of Hosts : tablets of Bahá'u'lláh.
        pages cm
    Includes bibliographical references and index.
    ISBN 978-1-61851-091-4 (alk. paper)
    1. Bahá'u'lláh, 1817–1892—Correspondence. 2. Bahai Faith—
Doctrines. I. Title.
    BP362.A3 2015
    297.9'3822—dc23
                                        2015021240

Cover design by Andrew Johnson
Book design by Patrick J. Falso

# CONTENTS

# PREFACE

The Bahá'í Faith is the youngest of the world's independent religions. Since its inception in Persia in the mid-nineteenth century it has since spread to virtually every corner of the earth. Today its membership represents what may well be the most ethnically and culturally diverse organized association of people. The growth of the Faith has been fueled by a body of teachings that its followers regard as the Revelation of God's guidance for the collective coming-of-age of humankind: the oneness of the human race, the oneness of the world's religions as the principal civilizing force in history, and the imperative challenge facing the earth's inhabitants to construct a global society based on principles of unity and justice.

Among the Faith's striking features is the fact that it owes its origin to the labors of two successive founding Prophets, the Báb and Bahá'u'lláh. As the former explained, His mission was to prepare the way for "Him Whom God shall make manifest," the Manifestation of God awaited by the followers of all faiths. During the course of successive waves of persecution that followed this announcement and that claimed the lives of the Báb and several thousands of His followers, Bahá'u'lláh declared Himself to be the fulfillment of the Divine promise. It is thus the voluminous body of the Latter's writings that constitutes the main corpus of Bahá'í scripture.

The rapid spread of the Faith today and the consequent rising public interest in its primary texts have prompted the decision to make available this edition of *The Summons of the Lord of Hosts,* which includes a glossary and some additional explanatory notes.

A word should perhaps be said about the literary style of the book's English translation. Bahá'u'lláh possessed a superlative command of classical Persian and Arabic, which He used as an instrument of transformative effect. His translators faced a daunting challenge, for their rendering had not only to convey precisely the Author's intent, but also to capture for the English reader the exalted and emotive spirit in which this intent was communicated. The form of expression settled upon—faithful in both respects to the original—is reminiscent of that used by seventeenth-century translators of the Bible, unique in its perennial power to touch the soul.

It gives us great pleasure to make available this edition of the several Tablets in which Bahá'u'lláh summoned the monarchs of East and West to recognize the Day of God and to acknowledge Him as the One promised in the scriptures of the world's religions.

THE NATIONAL SPIRITUAL ASSEMBLY OF
THE BAHÁ'ÍS OF THE UNITED STATES
NOVEMBER 2006

# INTRODUCTION

The years following Bahá'u'lláh's arrival in Adrianople witnessed His Revelation's attainment, in the words of Shoghi Effendi, of "its meridian glory" through the proclamation of its Founder's message to the kings and rulers of the world. During this relatively brief but turbulent period of the Faith's history, and in the early years of His subsequent exile in 1868 to the fortress town of 'Akká, He summoned the monarchs of East and West collectively, and some among them individually, to recognize the Day of God and to acknowledge the One promised in the scriptures of the religions professed by the recipients of His summons. "Never since the beginning of the world," Bahá'u'lláh declares, "hath the Message been so openly proclaimed."

The present volume brings together the first full, authorized English translation of these major writings. Among them is the complete Súriy-i-Haykal, the Súrih of the Temple, one of Bahá'u'lláh's most challenging works. It was originally revealed during His banishment to Adrianople and later recast after His arrival in 'Akká. In this version He incorporated His messages addressed to individual potentates—Pope Pius IX, Napoleon III, Czar Alexander II, Queen Victoria, and Násiri'd-Dín Sháh.

It was this composite work which, shortly after its completion, Bahá'u'lláh instructed be written in the form of a pentacle, symbolizing the human temple. To it He added, as a conclusion, what Shoghi Effendi has described as "words which reveal the importance He attached to those Messages, and indicate their direct association with the prophecies of the Old Testament":

Thus have We built the Temple with the hands of power and might, could ye but know it. This is the Temple promised unto you in the Book. Draw ye nigh unto it. This is that which profiteth you, could ye but comprehend it. Be fair, O peoples of the earth! Which is preferable, this, or a temple which is built of clay? Set your faces towards it. Thus have ye been commanded by God, the Help in Peril, the Self-Subsisting.

During the last years of His ministry Bahá'u'lláh Himself arranged for the publication for the first time of definitive versions of some of His principal works, and the Súriy-i-Haykal was awarded a prominent position among them.

Of the various writings that make up the Súriy-i-Haykal, one requires particular mention. The Lawh-i-Sulṭán, the Tablet to Náṣiri'd-Dín Sháh, Bahá'u'lláh's lengthiest epistle to any single sovereign, was revealed in the weeks immediately preceding His final banishment to 'Akká. It was eventually delivered to the monarch by Badí', a youth of seventeen, who had entreated Bahá'u'lláh for the honor of rendering some service. His efforts won him the crown of martyrdom and immortalized his name. The Tablet contains the celebrated passage describing the circumstances in which the divine call was communicated to Bahá'u'lláh and the effect it produced. Here, too, we find His unequivocal offer to meet with the Muslim clergy, in the presence of the Sháh, and to provide whatever proofs of the new Revelation they might consider to be definitive, a test of spiritual integrity significantly failed by those who claimed to be the authoritative trustees of the message of the Qur'án.

Included in this collection, as well, is the first full translation of the Súriy-i-Mulúk or Súrih of the Kings, which Shoghi Effendi described as "the most momentous Tablet revealed by Bahá'u'lláh in which He, for the first time, directs His words collectively to the entire company of the monarchs of East and West." It sets forth both the character of His mission and the standard of justice that must govern the exercise of their rule in this Day of God:

> Lay not aside the fear of God, O kings of the earth, and beware that ye transgress not the bounds which the Almighty hath fixed. Observe the injunctions laid upon you in His Book, and take good heed not to overstep their limits. Be vigilant, that ye may not do injustice to anyone, be it to the extent of a grain of mustard seed. Tread ye the path of justice, for this, verily, is the straight path.

The Tablet introduces some of the great themes that were to figure prominently in the Writings of Bahá'u'lláh over the next two and a half decades: the obligation of those into whose hands God has entrusted civil authority to institute the reign of justice, the necessity for the reduction of armaments and the resolution of conflicts among nations, and an end to the excessive expenditures that were impoverishing these rulers' subjects.

Surveying the principal contents of Bahá'u'lláh's majestic call to the kings and rulers of the world, Shoghi Effendi has written:

> The magnitude and diversity of the theme, the cogency of the argument, the sublimity and audacity of the language, arrest our attention and astound our minds. Emperors, kings and princes, chancellors and ministers, the Pope himself, priests, monks and philosophers, the exponents of learning, parliamentarians and deputies, the rich ones of the earth, the followers of all religions, and the people of Bahá—all are brought within the purview of the Author of these Messages, and receive, each according to their merits, the counsels and admonitions they deserve. No less amazing is the diversity of the subjects touched upon in these Tablets. The transcendent majesty and unity of an unknowable and unapproachable God is extolled, and the oneness of His Messengers proclaimed and emphasized. The uniqueness, the universality and potentialities of the Bahá'í Faith are stressed, and the purpose and character of the Bábí Revelation unfolded.

The summary draws attention to Bahá'u'lláh's uncompromising indictment of the conditions of human society for which its leadership is held primarily responsible:

> Episodes, at once moving and marvelous, at various stages of His ministry, are recounted, and the transito-

riness of worldly pomp, fame, riches, and sovereignty, repeatedly and categorically asserted. Appeals for the application of the highest principles in human and international relations are forcibly and insistently made, and the abandonment of discreditable practices and conventions, detrimental to the happiness, the growth, the prosperity and the unity of the human race, enjoined. Kings are censured, ecclesiastical dignitaries arraigned, ministers and plenipotentiaries condemned, and the identification of His advent with the coming of the Father Himself unequivocally admitted and repeatedly announced. The violent downfall of a few of these kings and emperors is prophesied, two of them are definitely challenged, most are warned, all are appealed to and exhorted.

In a Tablet, the original of which has been lost, Bahá'u'lláh had already condemned, in the severest terms, the misrule of the Ottoman Sulṭán 'Abdu'l-'Azíz. The present volume includes, however, three other Tablets which address two ministers of the Sulṭán, whose selfish and unprincipled influence played an important role in Bahá'u'lláh's successive banishments. The Súriy-i-Ra'ís, which addresses 'Alí Páshá, the Ottoman Prime Minister, was revealed in August 1868 as the exiles were being moved from Adrianople to Gallipoli, and exposes unsparingly the abuse of civil power the minister had perpetrated. The Lawḥ-i-Ra'ís, which also contains passages directed to 'Alí Páshá, was revealed shortly after Bahá'u'lláh's incarceration in the citadel of 'Akká and includes a chilling denunciation of the character of the minister. The third Tablet, the Lawḥ-i-Fu'ád, revealed in 1869 shortly after the death of Fu'ád Páshá, the Ottoman minister to whose machinations it refers, describes the spiritual consequences of the abuse of power, and foretells the imminent downfall of his colleague, 'Álí Páshá, and the overthrow of the Sulṭán himself—prophecies that were widely circulated and whose dramatic fulfillment added greatly to the prestige of their Author.

It seems especially appropriate, as Bahá'u'lláh's influence penetrates ever more deeply the life of the larger society throughout the world, that the full texts of these great Tablets should now be available for a broad readership. We express to the committees who were commissioned to undertake and review these translations the deep gratitude we feel for the care and sensitivity they have brought to the task. Bahá'ís will recognize key passages from several of the Tablets that were introduced to the West by Shoghi Effendi. His translations into English of the Bahá'í Holy Texts provide an enduring standard for the efforts of those who rise to the challenge of preparing appropriate renderings into English of these treasures of the Faith.

THE UNIVERSAL HOUSE OF JUSTICE

# SÚRIY-I-HAYKAL

*This is the Súrih of the Temple which God hath ordained to be the Mirror of His Names between the heavens and the earth, and the Sign of His Remembrance amidst the peoples*

## HE IS THE MOST WONDROUS, THE ALL-GLORIOUS!

Glorified is He Who hath revealed His verses to those who understand. Glorified is He Who revealeth His verses to those who perceive. Glorified is He Who guideth whomsoever He pleaseth unto His path. Say: I, verily, am the Path of God unto all who are in the heavens and all who are on the earth; well is it with them that hasten thereunto!

Glorified is He Who sendeth down His verses to those who comprehend. Glorified is He Who speaketh forth from the Kingdom of His Revelation, and Who remaineth unknown to all save His honored servants. Glorified is He Who quickeneth whomsoever He willeth by virtue of His word "Be," and it is! Glorified is He Who causeth whomsoever He willeth to ascend unto the heaven of grace, and sendeth down therefrom whatsoever He desireth according to a prescribed measure.

Blessed is He Who doeth as He willeth by a word of His command. He, verily, is the True One, the All-Knowing. Blessed is He Who inspireth whomsoever He willeth with whatsoever He desireth, through His irresistible and inscrutable command. Blessed is He Who aideth whomsoever He desireth with the hosts of the unseen. His might is, in truth, equal to His purpose, and He, verily, is the All-Glorious, the Self-Subsisting. Blessed is He Who exalteth whomsoever He willeth by the power of His sovereign might, and confirmeth whomsoever He chooseth in accordance with His good pleasure; well is it with them that understand!

4   Blessed is He Who, in a well-guarded Tablet, hath prescribed a fixed measure unto all things. Blessed is He Who hath revealed unto His Servant that which shall illumine the hearts and minds of men. Blessed is He Who hath sent down upon His Servant such tribulations as have melted the hearts of them that dwell within the Tabernacle of eternity and the souls of those who have drawn nigh unto their Lord. Blessed is He Who hath showered upon His Servant, from the clouds of His decree, the darts of affliction, and Who beholdeth Me enduring them with patience and fortitude. Blessed is He Who hath ordained for His Servant that which He hath destined for no other soul. He, verily, is the One, the Incomparable, the Self-Subsisting.

5   Blessed is He Who hath caused to rain down upon His Servant from the clouds of enmity, and at the hands of the people of denial, the shafts of tribulation and trial; and yet seeth Our heart filled with gratitude. Blessed is He Who hath laid upon the shoulders of His Servant the burden of the heavens and of the earth—a burden for which We yield Him every praise, though none may grasp this save them that are endued with understanding. Glorified is He Who hath surrendered the embodiment of His Beauty to the clutches of the envious and the wicked—a fate unto which We are fully resigned, though none may perceive this save

those who are endued with insight. Glorified is He Who hath left Ḥusayn to make His dwelling amidst the hosts of His enemies, and exposed His body with every breath to the spears of hatred and anger; yet do We yield Him thanks for all that He hath destined to befall His Servant Who repaireth unto Him in His affliction and grief.

While engulfed in tribulations I heard a most wondrous, a most sweet voice, calling above My head. Turning My face, I beheld a Maiden—the embodiment of the remembrance of the name of My Lord—suspended in the air before Me. So rejoiced was she in her very soul that her countenance shone with the ornament of the good pleasure of God, and her cheeks glowed with the brightness of the All-Merciful. Betwixt earth and heaven she was raising a call which captivated the hearts and minds of men. She was imparting to both My inward and outer being tidings which rejoiced My soul, and the souls of God's honored servants.

Pointing with her finger unto My head, she addressed all who are in heaven and all who are on earth, saying: By God! This is the Best-Beloved of the worlds, and yet ye comprehend not. This is the Beauty of God amongst you, and the power of His sovereignty within you, could ye but understand. This is the Mystery of God and His Treasure, the Cause of God and His glory unto all who are in the kingdoms of Revelation and of creation, if ye be of them that perceive. This is He Whose Presence is the ardent desire of the denizens of the Realm of eternity, and of them that dwell within the Tabernacle of glory, and yet from His Beauty do ye turn aside.

O people of the Bayán! If ye aid Him not, God will assuredly assist Him with the powers of earth and heaven, and sustain Him with the hosts of the unseen through His

6

7

8

3

command "Be," and it is! The day is approaching when God will have, by an act of His Will, raised up a race of men the nature of which is inscrutable to all save God, the All-Powerful, the Self-Subsisting. He shall purify them from the defilement of idle fancies and corrupt desires, shall lift them up to the heights of holiness, and shall cause them to manifest the signs of His sovereignty and might upon earth. Thus hath it been ordained by God, the All-Glorious, the All-Loving.

9    O people of the Bayán! Would ye deny Him Whose presence is the very object of your creation, while ye rejoice idly upon your couches? Would ye laugh to scorn and contend with Him, a single hair of Whose head exceleth, in the sight of God, all that are in the heavens and all that are on the earth? O people of the Bayán! Produce, then, that which ye possess, that I may know by what proof ye believed aforetime in the Manifestations of His Cause, and by what reason ye now wax so disdainful!

10    I swear by Him Who hath fashioned Me from the light of His own Beauty! None have I ever seen that surpasseth you in heedlessness or exceedeth you in blindness. Ye seek to prove your faith in God through such holy Tablets as ye possess, yet when the verses of God were revealed and His Lamp was lighted, ye disbelieved in Him Whose very Pen hath fixed the destinies of all things in the Preserved Tablet. Ye recite the sacred verses and yet repudiate Him Who is their Source and Revealer. Thus hath God blinded your eyes in requital for your deeds, would ye but understand. Day and night ye transcribe the verses of God, and yet ye remain shut out, as by a veil, from Him Who hath revealed them.

In this Day the Concourse on high beholdeth you in your 11
evil doings and shunneth your company, and yet ye perceive
it not. They ask of one another: "What words do these fools
utter, and in what valley are they wont to graze? Do they
deny that whereunto their very souls testify, and shut their
eyes to that which they plainly behold?" I swear by God, O
people! They that inhabit the Cities of the Names of God
are bewildered at your actions, while ye roam, aimless and
unconscious, in a parched and barren land.

O Pen of the Most High! Hearken unto the Call of Thy 12
Lord, raised from the Divine Lote-Tree in the holy and
luminous Spot, that the sweet accents of Thy Lord, the
All-Merciful, may fill Thy soul with joy and fervor, and that
the breezes that waft from My name, the Ever-Forgiving,
may dispel Thy cares and sorrows. Raise up, then, from this
Temple, the temples of the Oneness of God, that they may
tell out, in the kingdom of creation, the tidings of their
Lord, the Most Exalted, the All-Glorious, and be of them
that are illumined by His light.

We, verily, have ordained this Temple to be the source 13
of all existence in the new creation, that all may know of a
certainty My power to accomplish that which I have purposed through My word "Be," and it is! Beneath the shadow
of every letter of this Temple We shall raise up a people
whose number none can reckon save God, the Help in Peril,
the Self-Subsisting. Erelong shall God bring forth from His
Temple such souls as will remain unswayed by the insinua-
tions of the rebellious, and who will quaff at all times of the
cup that is life indeed. These, truly, are of the blissful.

These are servants who abide beneath the shelter of the 14
tender mercy of their Lord, and who remain undeterred by

those who seek to obstruct their path. Upon their faces may be seen the brightness of the light of the All-Merciful, and from their hearts may be heard the remembrance of Mine all-glorious and inaccessible Name. Were they to unloose their tongues to extol their Lord, the denizens of earth and heaven would join in their anthems of praise—yet how few are they who hear! And were they to glorify their Lord, all created things would join in their hymns of glory. Thus hath God exalted them above the rest of His creation, and yet the people remain unaware!

15     These are they who circle round the Cause of God even as the shadow doth revolve around the sun. Open, then, your eyes, O people of the Bayán, that haply ye may behold them! It is by virtue of their movement that all things are set in motion, and by reason of their stillness all things are brought to rest, would that ye might be assured thereof! Through them the believers in the Divine Unity have turned towards Him Who is the Object of the adoration of the entire creation, and by them the hearts of the righteous have found rest and composure, could ye but know it! Through them the earth hath been established, the clouds have rained down their bounty, and the bread of holiness hath descended from the heaven of grace, could ye but perceive it!

16     These souls are the protectors of the Cause of God on earth, who shall preserve its beauty from the obscuring dust stirred up by every rejected disbeliever. In the path of their Lord they shall not fear for their lives; rather will they sacrifice their all in their eagerness to behold the face of their Well-Beloved and His exaltation in this Name, the Almighty, the All-Powerful, the All-Glorious, the Most Holy.

17     O Living Temple! Arise by the power of Thy Self in such wise that all created things will be moved to arise with Thee.

Aid, then, Thy Lord through such ascendancy and might as We have bestowed upon Thee. Take heed lest Thou falter on that Day when all created things are filled with dismay; rather be Thou the revealer of My name, the Self-Subsisting. Assist Thy Lord to the utmost of Thine ability, and pay no heed to the peoples of the world, for that which their mouths utter is like unto the droning of a gnat in an endless valley. Quaff the water of life in My name, the All-Merciful, and proffer unto the near ones amongst the inmates of this heavenly garden that which shall cause them to become detached from all names and enter beneath this blessed and all-encompassing shadow.

O Living Temple! Through Thee have We gathered together all created things, whether in the heavens or on the earth, and called them to account for that which We had covenanted with them before the foundation of the world. And lo, but for a few radiant faces and eloquent tongues, We found most of the people dumbfounded, their eyes staring up in fear. From the former We brought forth the creation of all that hath been and all that shall be. These are they whose countenances God hath graciously turned away from the face of the unbelievers, and whom He hath sheltered beneath the shadow of the Tree of His own Being; they upon whose hearts He hath bestowed the gift of peace and tranquility, and whom He hath strengthened and assisted through the hosts of the seen and the unseen. 18

O Eyes of this Temple! Look not upon the heavens and that which they contain, nor upon the earth and them that dwell thereon, for We have created you to behold Our own Beauty: See it now before you! Withhold not your gaze therefrom, and deprive not yourselves of the Beauty of your Lord, the All-Glorious, the Best-Beloved. Erelong shall We 19 bring into being through you keen and penetrating eyes that will contemplate the manifold signs of their Creator and turn away from all that is perceived by the people of the world. Through you shall We bestow the power of vision upon whomsoever We desire, and lay hold upon those who have deprived themselves of this gracious bounty. These, verily, have drunk from the cup of delusion, though they perceive it not.

20    O Ears of this Temple! Purge yourselves from all idle clamor and hearken unto the melodies of your Lord. He, verily, revealeth unto you, from the Throne of glory, that there is none other God save Me, the All-Glorious, the Almighty, the Help in Peril, the Self-Subsisting. Erelong shall We bring into being through you pure and undefiled ears which will heed the Word of God and that which hath appeared from the Dayspring of the Utterance of your Lord, the All-Merciful. They shall assuredly perceive the sweet accents of Divine Revelation that proceed from these most blessed and hallowed precincts.

21    O Tongue of this Temple! We, verily, have created thee through Our name, the All-Merciful, have taught thee whatsoever had remained concealed in the Bayán, and have bestowed upon thee the power of utterance, that thou mayest make mention of Mine exalted Self amidst My creatures. Proclaim, then, this wondrous and mighty Remembrance, and fear not the manifestations of the Evil One. Thou wert called into being for this very purpose by virtue of My transcendent and all-compelling command. Through thee have We unloosed the Tongue of Utterance to expound all that

hath been, and We shall again, by My sovereign power, unloose it to speak of that which is yet to come. Erelong shall We bring into being through thee eloquent tongues that will praise and extol Me amongst the Concourse of eternity and amidst the peoples of the world. Thus have the verses of God been revealed, and thus hath it been decreed by the Lord of all names and attributes. Thy Lord, verily, is the True One, the Knower of things unseen. Nothing whatsoever shall prevent these tongues from magnifying their Creator. Through them, all created things shall arise to glorify the Lord of names and to bear witness that there is none other God save Me, the All-Powerful, the Most Glorious, the Best-Beloved. Nor shall those who make mention of Me speak aught unless they be inspired by this Tongue from its heavenly garden. Few, however, are they who understand! No tongue is there that speaketh not the praises of its Lord and maketh not mention of His Name. Amongst the people, however, are those who understand and utter praises, and those who utter praises, yet understand not.

O Maid of inner meanings! Step out of the chamber of 22 utterance by the leave of God, the Lord of the heavens and the earth. Reveal, then, thyself adorned with the raiment of the celestial Realm, and proffer with thy ruby fingers the wine of the heavenly Dominion, that haply the denizens of this world may perceive that the Daystar of eternity shone forth above the horizon of the Kingdom with the adornment of glory. Perchance they may arise before the dwellers of earth and heaven to extol and magnify this Youth Who hath established Himself in the midmost heart of Paradise upon the throne of His name, the Most Bountiful—He from Whose countenance shineth the brightness of the All-Merciful, from Whose gaze appear the glances of the All-Glorious, and in Whose ways are revealed the tokens and evidences of God, the Help in Peril, the Self-Subsisting.

23   Grieve not if none be found to accept the crimson wine proffered by Thy snow-white hand and to seize it in the name of Thy Lord, the Most Exalted, the Most High—He Who hath appeared again in His name, the Most Glorious. Leave this people unto themselves, and repair unto the Tabernacle of majesty and glory, wherein Thou shalt encounter a people whose faces shine as brightly as the sun in its noontide splendor, and who praise and extol their Lord in this Name that hath arisen, in the plenitude of might and power, to assume the throne of independent sovereignty. From their lips Thou shalt hear naught but the strains of My praise; unto this Thy Lord beareth Me witness. The existence of these people, however, hath remained concealed from the eyes of all who, from everlasting, have been created through the Word of God. Thus have We made plain Our meaning and set forth Our verses, that perchance men may reflect upon the signs and tokens of their Lord.

24   These are they who, in truth, were not enjoined to prostrate themselves before Adam.[1] They have never turned away from the countenance of Thy Lord, and partake at every moment of the gifts and delights of holiness. Thus hath the Pen of the All-Merciful set forth the secrets of all things, be they of the past or of the future. Would that the world might understand! Erelong shall God make manifest this people upon the earth, and through them shall exalt His name, diffuse His signs, uphold His words, and proclaim

His verses, in spite of those that have repudiated His truth, gainsaid His sovereignty, and caviled at His signs.

O Beauty of the All-Glorious! Shouldst Thou chance ²⁵ upon this people and enter their presence, recount unto them that which this Youth hath related unto Thee concerning Himself and the things that have befallen Him, that they may come to know what hath been inscribed upon the Preserved Tablet. Acquaint them with the tidings of this Youth, and with the trials and tribulations He hath suffered, that they may become mindful of Mine afflictions, and be of them that are occupied with His remembrance. Recount, then, unto them how We singled out for Our favor one of Our brothers,* how We imparted unto him a dewdrop from the fathomless ocean of knowledge, clothed him with the garment of one of Our Names, and exalted him to such a station that all were moved to extol him, and how We so protected him from the harm of the malevolent as to disarm even the mightiest amongst them.

We arose alone before the gaze of the peoples of earth and ²⁶ heaven at a time when all had determined to slay us. While dwelling in their midst, We continually made mention of the Lord, celebrated His praise, and stood firm in His Cause, until at last the Word of God was vindicated amongst His creatures, His signs were spread abroad, His power exalted, and His sovereignty revealed in its full splendor. To this bear witness all His honored servants. Yet when My brother beheld the rising fame of the Cause, he became filled with

* Mírzá Yaḥyá.

arrogance and pride. Thereupon he emerged from behind the veil of concealment, rose up against Me, disputed My verses, denied My testimony, and repudiated My signs. Nor would his hunger be appeased unless he were to devour My flesh and drink My blood. To this testify such of God's servants as have accompanied Him in His exile, and, beyond them, they that enjoy near access unto Him.

27     To this end he conferred with one of My servants[2] and sought to win him over to his own designs; whereupon the Lord dispatched unto Mine assistance the hosts of the seen and the unseen, protected Me by the power of truth, and sent down upon Me that which thwarted his purpose. Thus were foiled the plots of those who disbelieve in the verses of the All-Merciful. They, truly, are a rejected people. When news spread of that which the promptings of self had impelled My brother to attempt, and Our companions in exile learned of his nefarious design, the voice of their indignation and grief was lifted up and threatened to spread throughout the city. We forbade, however, such recriminations, and enjoined upon them patience, that they might be of those that endure steadfastly.

28     By God, besides Whom is none other God! We withstood all these trials with forbearance, and enjoined upon God's servants to show forth patience and fortitude. Removing Ourself from their midst, We took up residence in another house, that perchance the flame of envy might be quenched in Our brother's breast, and that he might be guided aright. We neither opposed him, nor saw him again thereafter, but remained in Our home, placing Our hopes in the bounty of God, the Help in Peril, the Self-Subsisting. When, however, he realized that his deed had been exposed, he seized the pen

of calumny and wrote unto the servants of God, attributing what he had himself committed unto Mine own peerless and wronged Beauty. His purpose was none other than to inspire mischief and to instill hatred into the hearts of those who had believed in God, the All-Glorious, the All-Loving.

By the One in Whose hand is My soul! We were dismayed by his deceitfulness—nay, bewildered were all things visible and invisible. Nor did he find respite from what he harbored in his bosom until he had committed that which no pen dare describe, and by which he disgraced the dignity of My station and profaned the sanctity of God, the Almighty, the All-Glorious, the All-Praised. Were God to turn all the oceans of the earth into ink and all created things into pens, they would not suffice Me to exhaust the record of his wrongdoings. Thus do We recount that which befell Us, that haply ye may be of them that understand. 29

O Pen of Eternity! Grieve not at the things that have befallen Thee, for erelong shall God raise up a people who will see with their own eyes and will recall Thy tribulations. Withhold Thy pen from the mention of Thine enemies, and bestir it in the praise of the Eternal King. Renounce all created things, and quaff the sealed wine of My remembrance. Beware lest Thou become occupied with the mention of those from whom naught save the noisome savors of enmity can be perceived, those who are so enslaved by their lust for leadership that they would not hesitate to destroy themselves in their desire to emblazon their fame and perpetuate their names. God hath recorded such souls in the Preserved Tablet as mere worshippers of names. Recount then that which Thou hast purposed for this Temple, that its signs and tokens may be made manifest upon earth, and 30 that the brightness of this Light may illumine the horizons of the world and cleanse the earth from the defilement of those who have disbelieved in God. Thus have We set down the verses of God and made plain the matter unto those who understand.

31     O Living Temple! Stretch forth Thy hand over all who are in heaven and on earth, and seize within the grasp of Thy Will the reins of command. We have, verily, placed in Thy right hand the empire of all things. Do as Thou willest, and fear not the ignorant. Reach out to the Tablet that hath dawned above the horizon of the pen of Thy Lord, and take hold of it in such wise that, through Thee, the hands of all who inhabit the earth may be enabled to lay fast hold upon it. This, in truth, is that which becometh Thee, if Thou be of those who understand. Through the upraising of Thy hand to the heaven of My grace, the hands of all created things shall be lifted up to their Lord, the Mighty, the Powerful, the Gracious. Erelong shall We raise up, through the aid of Thy hand, other hands endued with power, with strength and might, and shall establish through them Our dominion over all that dwell in the realms of revelation and creation. Thus will the servants of God recognize the truth that there is none other God beside Me, the Help in Peril, the Self-Subsisting. With these hands, moreover, We shall both bestow and withhold, though none can understand this save those who see with the eye of the spirit.

32     Say: O people! Can ye ever hope to escape the sovereign power of your Lord? By the righteousness of God! No refuge will ye find in this day, and no one to protect you, save those upon whom God hath bestowed the favor of His mercy. He, verily, is the Ever-Forgiving, the Most Compassionate. Say:

O people! Forsake all that ye possess, and enter beneath the shadow of your Lord, the All-Merciful. Better is this for you than all your works of the past and of the future. Fear ye God, and deprive not yourselves of the sweet savors of the days of God, the Lord of all names and attributes. Take heed lest ye alter or pervert the text of the Word of God. Walk ye in the fear of God, and be numbered with the righteous.

Say: O people! This is the Hand of God, which hath ever 33 been above your own hands, could ye but understand. Within its grasp We have ordained all the good of the heavens and the earth, such that no good shall be made manifest but that it proceedeth therefrom. Thus have We made it the source and treasury of all good both aforetime and hereafter. Say: The rivers of divine wisdom and utterance which flowed through the Tablets of God are joined to this Most Great Ocean, could ye but perceive it, and whatever hath been set forth in His Books hath attained its final consummation in this most exalted Word—a Word shining above the horizon of the Will of the All-Glorious in this Revelation which hath filled with delight all things seen and unseen.

Erelong shall God draw forth, out of the bosom of power, 34 the hands of ascendancy and might—hands who will arise to win victory for this Youth and who will purge mankind from the defilement of the outcast and the ungodly. These hands will gird up their loins to champion the Faith of God, and will, in My name the Self-Subsistent, the Mighty, subdue the peoples and kindreds of the earth. They will enter the cities and will inspire with fear the hearts of all their inhabitants. Such are the evidences of the might of God; how fearful, how vehement is His might, and how justly doth He wield it! He, verily, ruleth and transcendeth all who are in the heavens and on the earth, and revealeth what He desireth according to a prescribed measure.

35     Should any one of them be called upon to confront all the hosts of creation, he would assuredly prevail through the ascendancy of My Will. This, verily, is a proof of My power, though My creatures comprehend it not. This, verily, is a sign of My sovereignty, though My subjects understand it not. This, verily, is a token of My command, though My servants perceive it not. This, verily, is an evidence of Mine ascendancy, though none amongst the people is truly thankful for it, save those whose eyes God hath illumined with the light of His knowledge, whose hearts He hath made the repository of His Revelation, and upon whose shoulders He hath placed the weight of His Cause. These shall inhale the fragrances of the All-Merciful from the garment of His Name, and shall rejoice at all times in the signs and verses of their Lord. As for those who disbelieve in God, and join partners with Him, they shall indeed incur His wrath, shall be cast into the Fire, and shall be made to dwell, fearful and dismayed, in its depths. Thus do We expound Our verses, and make plain the truth with clear proofs, that perchance the people may reflect upon the signs of their Lord.

36     O Living Temple! We have, in very truth, appointed Thee to be the sign of My majesty amidst all that hath been and all that shall be, and have ordained Thee to be the emblem of My Cause betwixt the heavens and the earth, through My word "Be," and it is!

37     O First Letter of this Temple, betokening the Essence of Divinity![3] We have made thee the treasury of My Will and the repository of My Purpose unto all who are in the kingdoms of revelation and creation. This is but a token of the grace of Him Who is the Help in Peril, the Self-Subsisting.

O Second Letter of this Temple, betokening My name, the Almighty! We have made thee the manifestation of Our sovereignty and the dayspring of Our Names. Potent am I to fulfil that which My tongue speaketh.  38

O Third Letter of this Temple, betokening My name, the All-Bountiful! We have made thee the dawning-place of Our bounty amidst Our creatures and the fountainhead of Our generosity amidst Our people. Powerful am I in My dominion. Nothing whatsoever of all that hath been created in the heavens or on the earth can escape My knowledge, and I am the True One, the Knower of things unseen. 39

Send down out of the clouds of Thy generosity that which shall enrich all created things, and withhold not Thy favors from the world of being. Thou, verily, art the All-Bountiful in the heaven of Thine eternity, and the Lord of infinite grace unto all who inhabit the kingdom of names. Look not upon the people and the things they possess; look rather upon the wonders of Thy gifts and favors. Gather then Thy servants beneath Thy shade that shadoweth all mankind. Stretch forth the hand of bounty over all creation, and the fingers of bestowal over all existence. This, verily, is that which beseemeth Thee, though the people understand it not. Whosoever turneth his face towards Thee doeth so by Thy grace, and as to him who turneth away, Thy Lord, in truth, is independent of all created things. Unto this bear witness His true and devoted servants.  40

Erelong shall God raise up, through Thee, hands of indomitable strength and arms of invincible might, who will come forth from behind the veils, will render the All-Merciful victorious amongst the peoples of the world, and will raise so mighty a cry as to cause all hearts to tremble with fear. Thus hath it been decreed in a Written Tablet. Such shall be 41 the ascendancy which these souls will evince that consternation and dismay will seize all the dwellers of the earth.

42     Beware lest ye shed the blood of anyone. Unsheathe the sword of your tongue from the scabbard of utterance, for therewith ye can conquer the citadels of men's hearts. We have abolished the law to wage holy war against each other. God's mercy, hath, verily, encompassed all created things, if ye do but understand. Aid ye your Lord, the God of Mercy, with the sword of understanding. Keener indeed is it, and more finely tempered, than the sword of utterance, were ye but to reflect upon the words of your Lord. Thus have the hosts of Divine Revelation been sent down by God, the Help in Peril, the Self-Subsisting, and thus have the armies of divine inspiration been made manifest from the Source of command, as bidden by God, the All-Glorious, the Best-Beloved.

43     Say: The measure of all created things hath been appointed in this concealed and manifest Temple, wherein lie enshrined the knowledge of the heavens and the earth, and of all things past and future. The finger of God's handiwork hath inscribed upon this Tablet that which the wisest and most learned of men are powerless to fathom, and hath created therein temples inscrutable to all save His own Self, could ye but apprehend this truth. Blessed be the one who readeth it, who pondereth its contents, and who is numbered with them that comprehend!

44     Say: Naught is seen in My temple but the Temple of God, and in My beauty but His Beauty, and in My being but His Being, and in My self but His Self, and in My movement but His Movement, and in My acquiescence but His Ac-

quiescence, and in My pen but His Pen, the Mighty, the All-Praised. There hath not been in My soul but the Truth, and in Myself naught could be seen but God.

Beware lest ye speak of duality in regard to My Self, 45 for all the atoms of the earth proclaim that there is none other God but Him, the One, the Single, the Mighty, the Loving. From the beginning that hath no beginning I have proclaimed, from the realm of eternity, that I am God, none other God is there save Me, the Help in Peril, the Self-Subsisting; and unto the end that hath no end I shall proclaim, amidst the kingdom of names, that I am God, none other God is there beside Me, the All-Glorious, the Best-Beloved. Say: Lordship is My Name, whereof I have created manifestations in the world of being, while We Ourself remain sanctified above them, would ye but ponder this truth. And Godhead is My Name, whereof We have created exponents whose power shall encompass the people of the earth and make them true worshippers of God, could ye but recognize it. Thus should ye regard all Our Names, if ye be endued with insight.

O Fourth Letter of this Temple, betokening the attribute 46 of Grace! We have made thee the manifestation of grace betwixt earth and heaven. From thee have We generated all grace in the contingent world, and unto thee shall We cause it to return. And from thee shall We manifest it again, through a word of Our command. Potent am I to accomplish whatsoever I desire through My word "Be," and it is! Every grace that appeareth in the world of being hath originated from thee, and unto thee shall it return. This, verily, is what hath been ordained in a Tablet which We have preserved behind the veil of glory and concealed from mortal eyes. Well is it with them that deprive themselves not of this conferred and unfailing grace.

47    Say: In this day, the fertilizing winds of the grace of God have passed over all things. Every creature hath been endowed with all the potentialities it can carry. And yet the peoples of the world have denied this grace! Every tree hath been endowed with the choicest fruits, every ocean enriched with the most luminous gems. Man, himself, hath been invested with the gifts of understanding and knowledge. The whole creation hath been made the recipient of the revelation of the All-Merciful, and the earth the repository of things inscrutable to all except God, the Truth, the Knower of things unseen. The time is approaching when every created thing will have cast its burden. Glorified be God Who hath vouchsafed this grace that encompasseth all things, whether seen or unseen! Thus have We created the whole earth anew in this day, yet most of the people have failed to perceive it. Say: The grace of God can never be adequately understood; how much less can His own Self, the Help in Peril, the Self-Subsisting, be comprehended!

48    O Temple of the Cause! Grieve not if Thou findest none ready to receive Thy gifts. Thou wast created for My sake; occupy Thyself therefore with My praise amidst My servants. This is that which hath been ordained for Thee in the Preserved Tablet. Having found upon the earth many a soiled hand, We sanctified the hem of Thy garment from the profanity of their touch and placed it beyond the reach of the ungodly. Be patient in the Cause of Thy Lord, for erelong shall He raise up sanctified hearts and illumined eyes who shall flee from every quarter unto Thine all-encompassing and boundless grace.

O Temple of God! No sooner had the hosts of Divine    49
Revelation been sent down by the Lord of all names and attributes bearing the banners of His signs, than the exponents
of doubt and fancy were put to flight. They disbelieved in
the clear tokens of God, the Help in Peril, the Self-Subsisting, and rose up against Him in enmity and opposition.
Amongst them were those who claimed: "These are not clear
verses from God, nor do they proceed from an innate and
untaught nature." Thus do the unbelievers seek to remedy
the sickness of their hearts, utterly heedless that they thus
render themselves accursed of all who dwell in heaven and
on earth.

Say: The Holy Spirit Itself hath been generated through    50
the agency of a single letter revealed by this Most Great
Spirit, if ye be of them that comprehend. And that innate
and untaught nature in its essence is called into being by
the verses of God, the Help in Peril, the All-Glorious, the
Best-Beloved. Say: This nature prideth itself in its relation
to Our transcendent Truth, whilst We, for Our part, glory
neither in it nor in aught else, for all beside Myself hath
been created through the potency of My word, could ye but
understand.

Say : We have revealed Our verses in nine different modes.    51
Each one of them bespeaketh the sovereignty of God, the
Help in Peril, the Self-Subsisting. A single one of them suf-
ficeth for a proof unto all who are in the heavens and on
the earth; yet the people, for the most part, persist in their
heedlessness. Should it be Our wish, We would reveal them
in countless other modes.

Say: O people! Fear ye God, and allow not your tongues    52
to utter, in their deceitfulness, that which displeaseth Him.

Stand abashed before the One Who, as ye well know, hath created you out of a drop of water.[4] Say: We have created all that are in heaven and on earth in the nature made by God. Whosoever turneth unto this blessed Countenance shall manifest the potentialities of that inborn nature, and whosoever remaineth veiled therefrom shall be deprived of this invisible and all-encompassing grace. Verily, there is naught from which Our favor hath been withheld, inasmuch as We have dealt equitably in the fashioning of each and all, and by a word of Our mouth presented unto them the trust of Our love. They that have accepted it are indeed safe and secure, and are numbered among those who are immune from the terrors of this Day. Those, however, who have rejected it have, in truth, disbelieved in God, the Help in Peril, the Self-Subsisting. Thus do We distinguish between the people and pronounce judgment upon them. We, of a certainty, have the power to discern.

53    Say: The Word of God can never be confounded with the words of His creatures. It is, in truth, the King of words, even as He is Himself the sovereign Lord of all, and His Cause transcendeth all that was and all that shall be. Enter, O people, the City of Certitude wherein the throne of your Lord, the All-Merciful, hath been established. Thus biddeth you the Pen of the All-Glorious, as a token of His unfailing grace. Haply ye may not make His Revelation a cause of dissension amongst you.

54    Among the infidels are those who have repudiated His Self and risen up against His Cause, and who claim that these divine verses are contrived. Such also were the objections of the deniers of old, who now implore deliverance from the Fire. Say: Woe betide you for the idle words that proceed

from your mouths! If these verses be indeed contrived, then by what proof have ye believed in God? Produce it, if ye be men of understanding! Whensoever We revealed Our clear verses unto such men, they rejected them, and whensoever they beheld that which the combined forces of the earth are powerless to produce, they pronounced it sorcery.

What aileth this people that they speak of that which they understand not? They raise the same objections as did the followers of the Qur'án when their Lord came unto them with His Cause. They, verily, are a rejected people. They hindered others from appearing before Him Who is the Ancient Beauty, and from sharing the bread of His loved ones. "Approach them not," one was even heard to say, "for they cast a spell upon the people and lead them astray from the path of God, the Help in Peril, the Self-Subsisting." By the righteousness of the one true God! He who is incapable of speaking in Our presence is uttering such words as none among the former generations hath ever spoken, and hath committed such acts as none of the unbelievers of bygone ages hath ever committed. 55

The very words and deeds of these men bear eloquent testimony to the truth of My words, if ye be of them that judge with fairness. Whosoever attributeth the verses of God to sorcery hath not believed in any of His Messengers, hath lived and labored in vain, and is accounted of those who speak that of which they have no knowledge. Say: O servant! Fear God, thy Creator and thy Fashioner, and transgress not against Him, but judge with fairness and act with justice. Those whom the Lord hath endued with knowledge shall find, in the very objections raised by the unbelievers, conclusive proofs to invalidate their claims and vindicate 56 the truth of this manifest Light. Say: Would ye repeat that which the unbelievers uttered when a Message came unto them from their Lord? Woe betide you, O assemblage of foolish ones, and blighted be your works!

57    O Ancient Beauty! Turn aside from the unbelievers and that which they possess, and waft over all created things the sweet savors of the remembrance of Thy Beloved, the Exalted, the Great. This remembrance quickeneth the world of being and reneweth the temples of all created things. Say: He, verily, hath established Himself upon the Throne of might and glory. Whosoever desireth to gaze upon His countenance, lo, behold Him standing before thee! Blessed be the Lord Who hath revealed Himself in this shining and luminous Beauty. Whosoever desireth to hearken unto His melodies, lo, hear them rising from His resplendent and wondrous lips! And unto whosoever desireth to be illumined by the splendors of His light, say: Seek the court of His presence, for God hath verily granted you leave to approach it, as a token of His grace unto all mankind.

58    Say: O people! We shall put to you a question in all truthfulness, taking God for a witness between you and Us. He, verily, is the Defender of the righteous. Appear, then, before His Throne of glory and make reply with justice and fair-mindedness. Is it God Who is potent to achieve His purpose, or is it ye who enjoy such authority? Is it He Who is truly unconstrained, as ye imply when ye say that He doeth what He pleaseth and shall not be asked of His doings, or is it ye who wield such power, and who merely make such assertions out of blind imitation, as did your forebears at the appearance of every other Messenger of God?

59    If He be truly unconstrained, behold then how He hath sent down the Manifestation of His Cause with verses which

naught in the heavens or on the earth can withstand! Such hath been the manner of their revelation that they have neither peer nor likeness in the world of being, as ye yourselves beheld and heard when once the Daystar of the world shone forth above the horizon of 'Iráq with manifest dominion. All things attain their consummation in the divine verses, and these indeed are the verses of God, the Sovereign Lord, the Help in Peril, the All-Glorious, the Almighty. Beyond this, He hath been made manifest as the Bearer of a Cause whose sovereign might is acknowledged by all created things, and this none can deny save the sinners and the ungodly.

Say: O people! Is it your wish to conceal the beauty of the  60
Sun behind the veils of your own selfish desires, or to prevent the Spirit from raising its melodies within this sanctified and luminous breast? Fear ye God, and contend not with Him Who representeth the Godhead. Dispute not with the One at Whose bidding the letter "B" was created and joined with its mighty foundation.[5] Believe in the Messengers of God and His sovereign might, and in the Self of God and His majesty. Follow not those who have repudiated what they had once believed, and who have sought for themselves a station after their own fancy; these, truly, are of the ungodly. Bear ye witness unto that whereunto God Himself hath borne witness, that the company of His favored ones may be illumined by the words that issue from your lips. Say: We, verily, believe in that which was revealed unto the Apostles of old, in that which hath been revealed, by the power of truth, unto 'Alí,* and in that which is now being revealed from His Throne of glory. Thus doth your Lord instruct

---

* The Báb.

you, as a sign of His favor and as a token of His grace that encompasseth all the worlds.

61    O Feet of this Temple! We, verily, have wrought you of iron. Stand firm with such constancy in the Cause of your Lord as to cause the feet of every severed soul to be strengthened in the path of God, the Almighty, the All-Wise. Beware lest the storms of enmity and hatred, or the blasts of the workers of iniquity, cause you to stumble. Be immovable in the Faith of God, and waver not. We, verily, have called you forth by virtue of that Name which is the source of all steadfastness, and by the grace of each one of Our most excellent Names as revealed unto all who are in heaven and on earth. Erelong shall We bring into being through you other feet, firm and steadfast, which shall walk unwaveringly in Our path, even should they be assailed by hosts as formidable as the combined forces of the former and latter generations. In truth, We hold all grace in the hollow of Our hand, and bestow it as We please upon Our favored servants. Time and again have We vouchsafed unto you Our favors, that ye may offer such thanks unto your Lord as to cause the tongues of all created things to speak forth in praise of Me, the All-Merciful, the Most Compassionate.

62    Arise to serve this Cause through a might and a power born of Us. Disclose, then, unto the servants of God all that the Spirit of God, the sovereign Lord, the Incomparable, the All-Glorious, the All-Wise, hath imparted unto Thee. Say: O people! Will ye turn away from Him Who is the Eternal Truth, and choose instead him whom We have created out of a mere handful of clay? To do so is to inflict a grievous injustice upon yourselves, if ye be of them that reflect upon the verses of your Lord. Say: O people! Cleanse your hearts

and your eyes, that ye may recognize your Maker in this holy and luminous attire. Say: The celestial Youth hath ascended the Throne of glory, made manifest His independent sovereignty, and now voiceth, in the most sweet and wondrous accents, this call betwixt earth and heaven: "O peoples of the earth! Wherefore have ye disbelieved in your Lord, the All-Merciful, and turned aside from Him Who is the Beauty of the All-Glorious? By the righteousness of God! This is His Hidden Secret, Who hath risen from the dayspring of creation; and this is His cherished Beauty, Who hath shone forth above the horizon of this heavenly garden, invested with the sovereignty of God, the Help in Peril, the All-Glorious, the All-Subduing, the Almighty."

O Temple of Holiness! We, verily, have cleansed Thy 63 breast from the whisperings of the people and sanctified it from earthly allusions, that the light of My beauty may appear therein and be reflected in the mirrors of all the worlds. Thus have We singled Thee out above all that hath been created in the heavens and the earth, and above all that hath been decreed in the realms of revelation and creation, and chosen Thee for Our own Self. This is but an evidence of the bounty which God hath vouchsafed unto Thee, a bounty which shall last until the Day that hath no end in this contingent world. It shall endure so long as God, the Supreme King, the Help in Peril, the Mighty, the Wise, shall endure. For the Day of God is none other but His own Self, Who hath appeared with the power of truth. This is the Day that shall not be followed by night, nor shall it be bounded by any praise, would that ye might understand!

O Breast of this Temple! We, verily, have caused all things 64 to mirror forth thy reality, and made thee as a mirror of Our own Self. Shed, then, upon the breasts of all created beings the splendors of the light of thy Lord, that they may be freed from all allusions and limitations. Thus hath the Daystar of wisdom shone forth above the horizon of the Pen of the Eternal King. Blessed are those who perceive it! Through thee have We created other sanctified breasts, and unto thee shall We cause them to return, as a token of Our grace unto thee and unto Our favored servants. Erelong shall We bring into being through thee men with sanctified and illumined breasts, who will testify to naught save My beauty and show forth naught but the resplendent light of My countenance. These shall in truth be the mirrors of My Names amidst all created things.

65       O Temple of Holiness! We, verily, have made Thine inmost heart the treasury of all the knowledge of past and future ages, and the dawning-place of Our own knowledge which We have ordained for the dwellers of earth and heaven, that all creation may partake of the outpourings of Thy grace and may attain, through the wonders of Thy knowledge, unto the recognition of God, the Exalted, the Powerful, the Great. In truth, that knowledge which belongeth unto Mine own Essence is such as none hath ever attained or will ever grasp, nor shall any heart be capable of bearing its weight. Were but a single word of this knowledge to be disclosed, the hearts of all men would be filled with consternation, the foundations of all things would crumble into ruin, and the feet of even the wisest among men would be made to slip.

66       Within the treasury of Our Wisdom there lieth unrevealed a knowledge, one word of which, if we chose to divulge it to mankind, would cause every human being to

recognize the Manifestation of God and to acknowledge His omniscience, would enable every one to discover the secrets of all the sciences, and to attain so high a station as to find himself wholly independent of all past and future learning. Other knowledges We do as well possess, not a single letter of which We can disclose, nor do We find humanity able to hear even the barest reference to their meaning. Thus have We informed you of the knowledge of God, the All-Knowing, the All-Wise. Were We to find worthy vessels, We would impart unto them the treasures of hidden meanings and apprise them of a knowledge, one letter of which would encompass all created things.

O Inmost Heart of this Temple! We have made thee the 67 dawning-place of Our knowledge and the dayspring of Our wisdom unto all who are in heaven and on earth. From thee have We caused all sciences to appear, and unto thee shall We cause them to return. And from thee shall We bring them forth a second time. Such, indeed, is Our promise, and potent are We to effect Our purpose. Erelong shall We bring into being through thee exponents of new and wondrous sciences, of potent and effective crafts, and shall make manifest through them that which the heart of none of Our servants hath yet conceived. Thus do We bestow upon whom We will whatsoever We desire, and thus do We withdraw from whom We will what We had once bestowed. Even so do We ordain whatsoever We please through Our behest.

Say: Should We choose, at one time, to shed the radiance 68 of Our loving providence upon the mirrors of all things, and, at another, to withhold from them the splendors of Our light, this verily lieth within Our power, and none hath the right to ask "why" or "wherefore." For We are potent indeed to achieve Our purpose, and render no account for that which We bring to pass; and none can doubt this save those who join partners with God and question His Truth. Say: Nothing can withstand the power of Our might or interrupt the course of Our command. We exalt whomsoever We please unto the Realm of supernal might and glory, and, should We so desire, cause the same to sink into the lowest abyss of degradation.

69   O dwellers of the earth! Would ye contend that if We raise up a soul unto the Sadratu'l-Muntahá,[6] it shall then cease to be subject to the power of Our sovereignty and dominion? Nay, by Mine own Self! Should it be Our wish, We would return it to the dust in less than the twinkling of an eye. Consider a tree: Behold how We plant it in a garden, and nourish it with the waters of Our loving care; and how, when it hath grown tall and mature, and brought forth verdant leaves and goodly fruits, lo, We send forth the tempestuous gales of Our decree, and lay it uprooted and prostrate upon the face of the earth. So hath it been Our way with all things, and so shall it be in this day. Such, in truth, are the matchless wonders of Our immutable method—a method which hath ever governed, and shall continue to govern, all things, if ye be of them that perceive. None, however, knoweth the wisdom thereof save God, the All-Powerful, the Almighty, the All-Wise.

70   Would ye gainsay, O people, the very thing that your eyes behold? Woe unto you, O assemblage of deniers! That which alone is exempt from change is His own Self, the All-Merciful, the Most Compassionate, were ye to gaze with the eye of insight, while all else beside Him can be altered

by an act of His Will. He, verily, is the All-Powerful, the Almighty, the All-Wise.

O people! Dispute not concerning My Cause, for ye shall never fathom the manifold wisdom of your Lord, nor shall ye ever gauge the knowledge of Him Who is the All-Glorious, the All-Pervading. Whosoever layeth claim to have known His Essence is without doubt among the most ignorant of all people. Every atom in the universe would charge such a man with imposture, and to this beareth witness My tongue which speaketh naught but the truth. Magnify My Cause and promulgate My teachings and commandments, for none other course beside this shall beseem you, and no other path shall ever lead unto Him. Would that ye might heed Our counsel! 71

O Living Temple! We have made Thee the Dayspring of each one of Our most excellent titles, the Dawning-Place of each one of Our most august attributes, and the Fountain-head of each one of Our manifold virtues unto the denizens of earth and heaven. Thereafter have We raised Thee up in Our own image betwixt the heavens and the earth, and ordained Thee to be the sign of Our glory unto all who are in the realms of revelation and creation, that My servants may follow in Thy footsteps, and be of them who are guided aright. We have appointed Thee the Tree of grace and bounty unto the dwellers of both the heavens and the earth. Well is it with them who seek the shelter of Thy shade and who draw nigh unto Thy Self, the omnipotent Protector of the worlds. 72

Say: We have made each one of Our Names a wellspring from which We have caused the streams of divine wisdom and understanding to gush forth and flow in the garden of 73

Our Cause—streams whose number none can reckon save Thy Lord, the Most Holy, the Omnipotent, the Omniscient, the All-Wise. Say: We have generated all Letters from the Point and have caused them to return unto It, and We have sent It down again in the form of a human temple. All glory be unto the Author of this incomparable and wondrous handiwork! Erelong shall We unfold and expound It again, in Our name, the All-Glorious. This is indeed a token of Our grace, and I, truly, am the Most Bountiful, the Ancient of Days.

74    We have brought forth all Lights from the Orb of Our name, the True One, have caused them to return unto It, and have again made them manifest in the form of a human temple. All glory be unto the Lord of strength, might, and power! None can withstand the operation of My will or the exercise of My might. I am He Who hath raised up all creatures through a word of My mouth, and My power is, in truth, equal to My purpose.

75    Say: It is in Our power, should We wish it, to cause all created things to expire in an instant, and, with the next, to endue them again with life. The knowledge thereof, however, is with God alone, the All-Knowing, the All-Informed. It is in Our power, should We wish it, to enable a speck of floating dust to generate, in less than the twinkling of an eye, suns of infinite, of unimaginable splendor, to cause a dewdrop to develop into vast and numberless oceans, to infuse into every letter such a force as to empower it to unfold all the knowledge of past and future ages. This, in truth, is a matter simple of accomplishment. Such have been the evidences of My power from the beginning that hath no beginning until the end that hath no end. My creatures,

however, have been oblivious of My power, have repudiated My sovereignty, and contended with Mine own Self, the All-Knowing, the All-Wise.

Say: Of all that lieth between heaven and earth, naught 76 can stir except by My leave, and unto My Kingdom none can ascend save at My behest. My creatures, however, have remained veiled from My might and My sovereignty, and are numbered with the heedless. Say: Naught is seen in My revelation but the Revelation of God, and in My might but His Might, could ye but know it. Say: My creatures are even as the leaves of a tree. They proceed from the tree, and depend upon it for their existence, yet remain oblivious of their root and origin. We draw such similitudes for the sake of Our discerning servants that perchance they may transcend a mere plant-like level of existence and attain unto true maturity in this resistless and immovable Cause. Say: My creatures are even as the fish of the deep. Their life dependeth upon the water, and yet they remain unaware of that which, by the grace of an omniscient and omnipotent Lord, sustaineth their very existence. Indeed, their heedlessness is such that were they asked concerning the water and its properties, they would prove entirely ignorant. Thus do We set forth comparisons and similitudes, that perchance the people may turn unto Him Who is the Object of the adoration of the entire creation.

O people! Fear God, and disbelieve not in Him Whose 77 grace hath surrounded all things, Whose mercy hath pervaded the contingent world, and the sovereign potency of Whose Cause hath encompassed both your inner and your outer beings, both your beginning and your end. Stand ye in awe of the Lord, and be of them that act uprightly. Beware lest ye be accounted among those who allow the verses of their Lord to pass them by unheard and unrecognized; these, truly, are of the wayward.

78      Say: Would ye worship him who neither heareth nor seeth, and who is of a truth the most abject and wayward of all God's servants? Wherefore have ye failed to follow the One Who hath come unto you from the Source of Divine Command bearing the tidings of God, the Most Exalted, the Most Great? O people! Be not like unto those who entered before Our throne, and yet failed to perceive or comprehend; these are indeed a contemptible people. We recited unto them verses that would enrapture the dwellers of the heavenly Dominion and the inmates of the Kingdom on high, and yet they departed veiled therefrom, and hearkened rather unto the voice of him who is but a servant of God and a mere creation of His Will. Thus do We impart unto you that which shall guide you towards the path of God's favored ones.

79      How many those who entered within the Abode of Paradise, the Seat wherein the throne of God had been established, and stood before their Lord, the Most Exalted, the Most Great, only to inquire about the four Gates or of some Imám of the Islamic Faith![7] Such was the state of these souls, if ye be of them that comprehend. It is even as ye witness in the present day: Those who have disbelieved in God and joined partners with Him cling to a single one of Our Names, and are debarred from recognizing Him Who is the Creator of all Names. We testify that such men are of a truth amongst the people of the Fire. They ask the sun to expound the words of the shadow, and the True One to explain the utterances of His creatures, could ye but perceive it! Say: O people! The sun offereth naught save the effulgence of its

own light and that which appeareth therefrom, whilst all else seek illumination from its rays. Fear God, and be not of the ignorant! Among them also were those who inquired of the darkness about the light. Say: Open thine eyes, that thou mayest behold the brightness which hath visibly enveloped the earth! This, verily, is a light which hath risen and shone forth above the horizon of the Dayspring of divine knowledge with manifest radiance. Would ye ask the Jews whether Jesus was the True One from God, or the idols if Muḥammad was an Apostle of His Lord, or inquire from the people of the Qur'án as to Him Who was the Remembrance of God, the Most Exalted, the Most Great?

Say: O people! Cast away, before the splendors of this Revelation, the things that ye possess, and cleave to that which God hath bidden you observe. Such is His command unto you, and He, verily, is best able to command. By My Beauty! By those words which I have revealed, Myself is not intended, but rather He Who will come after Me. To it is witness God, the All-Knowing. Deal not with Him as ye have dealt with Me. Do not object, when the verses of God are sent down unto you from the Court of My favor, saying, "these do not proceed from an innate and untaught nature," for that nature itself hath been created by My word and circleth round Me, if ye be of them that apprehend this truth. Inhale from the utterances of your Lord, the All-Merciful, the sweet smell of the garment of inner meanings, which hath been diffused throughout the entire creation and hath shed its fragrance over all created things. Happy are those who perceive it and hasten unto God with radiant hearts.

O Living Temple! We, verily, have made Thee a mirror unto the kingdom of names, that Thou mayest be, amidst all mankind, a sign of My sovereignty, a herald unto My

80

81

35

presence, a summoner unto My beauty, and a guide unto My straight and perspicuous Path. We have exalted Thy Name among Our servants as a bounty from Our presence. I, verily, am the All-Bountiful, the Ancient of Days. We have, moreover, adorned Thee with the ornament of Our own Self, and have imparted unto Thee Our Word, that Thou mayest ordain in this contingent world whatsoever Thou willest and accomplish whatsoever Thou pleasest. We have destined for Thee all the good of the heavens and of the earth, and decreed that none may attain unto a portion thereof unless he entereth beneath Thy shadow, as bidden by Thy Lord, the All-Knowing, the All-Informed. We have conferred upon Thee the Staff of authority and the Writ of judgment, that Thou mayest test the wisdom of every command. We have caused the oceans of inner meaning and explanation to surge from Thy heart in remembrance of Thy Lord, the God of mercy, that Thou mayest render thanks and praise unto Him and be of those who are truly thankful. We have singled Thee out from amongst all Our creatures, and have appointed Thee as the Manifestation of Our own Self unto all who are in the heavens and on the earth.

82    Bring then into being, by Our leave, resplendent mirrors and exalted letters that shall testify to Thy sovereignty and dominion, bear witness to Thy might and glory, and be the manifestations of Thy Names amidst mankind. We have caused Thee again to be the Origin and the Creator of all mirrors, even as We brought them forth from Thee aforetime. And We shall cause Thee to return unto Mine own Self, even as We called Thee forth in the beginning. Thy Lord, verily, is the Unconstrained, the All-Powerful, the

All-Compelling. Warn, then, these mirrors, once they have been made manifest, lest they swell with pride before their Creator and Fashioner when He appeareth amongst them, or let the trappings of leadership debar them from bowing in submission before God, the Almighty, the All-Beauteous.

Say: O concourse of mirrors! Ye are but a creation of My will and have come to exist by virtue of My command. Beware lest ye deny the verses of My Lord, and be of them who have wrought injustice and are numbered with the lost. Beware lest ye cling unto that which ye possess, or take pride in your fame and renown. That which behooveth you is to wholly detach yourselves from all that is in the heavens and on the earth. Thus hath it been ordained by Him Who is the All-Powerful, the Almighty. 83

O Temple of My Cause! Say: Should I wish to transform, in a single moment, all things into mirrors of My Names, this undoubtedly is in My power, how much more in the power of My Lord, Who hath called Me into being through His all-compelling and inscrutable command. And should I choose to revolutionize the entire creation in the twinkling of an eye, this assuredly is possible unto Me, how much more unto that sovereign Purpose enshrined in the Will of God, My Lord and the Lord of all the worlds. 84

Say: O ye manifestations of My Names! Should ye offer up all that ye possess, nay your very lives, in the path of God, and invoke Him to the number of the grains of sand, the drops of rain, and the waves of the sea, and yet oppose the Manifestation of His Cause at the time of His appearance, your works shall in no wise be mentioned before God. Should ye, however, neglect all righteous works and yet choose to believe in Him in these days, God perchance will 85 put away your sins. He, verily, is the All-Glorious, the Most Bountiful. Thus doth the Lord inform you of His purpose, that haply ye may not wax proud before the One through Whom whatsoever hath been revealed from all eternity hath been confirmed. Happy is he who approacheth this Most Sublime Vision, and woe to them that turn aside!

86     How numerous those who expend all their wealth in the path of God, and whom We find, at the hour of His Revelation, to be of the rebellious and the froward! How many those who keep the fast in the daytime, only to protest against the One by Whose very command the ordinance of the fast was first established! Such men are, in truth, of the ignorant. And how many those who subsist on the coarsest bread, who take for their only seat the grass of the field, and who undergo every manner of hardship, merely to maintain their superiority in the eyes of men! Thus do We expose their deeds, that this may serve as a warning unto others. These are the ones who subject themselves to all manner of austerities before the gaze of others in the hope of perpetuating their names, whilst in reality no mention shall remain of them save in the curses and imprecations of the dwellers of earth and heaven.

87     Say: Would it profit you in the least if, as ye fondly imagine, your names were to endure? Nay, by the Lord of all worlds! Was the idol 'Uzzá[8] made any greater by this, that its name lived on amidst the worshippers of names? Nay, by Him Who is the Self of God, the All-Glorious, the All-Compelling! Should your names fade from every mortal mind, and yet God be well pleased with you, ye will indeed be numbered among the treasures of His name, the Most Hidden. Thus have We sent down Our verses that they may

attract you unto the Source of all Lights, and acquaint you with the purpose of your Lord, the All-Knowing, the All-Wise. Abstain, then, from all that hath been forbidden unto you in the Book, and eat of the lawful things which God hath provided for your sustenance. Deprive not yourselves of His goodly bestowals, for He, verily, is the Most Generous, the Lord of grace abounding. Subject not yourselves to excessive hardships, but follow the way We have made plain unto you through Our luminous verses and perspicuous proofs, and be not of the negligent.

O concourse of divines! It is not yours to boast if ye abstain from drinking wine and from similar transgressions which have been forbidden you in the Book, for should ye commit such deeds, the dignity of your station would then be tainted in the eyes of the people, your affairs would be disrupted, and your name disgraced and dishonored. Nay, your true and abiding glory resideth in submission to the Word of Him Who is the Eternal Truth, and in your inward and outward detachment from aught else besides God, the All-Compelling, the Almighty. Great is the blessedness of that divine that hath not allowed knowledge to become a veil between him and the One Who is the Object of all knowledge, and who, when the Self-Subsisting appeared, hath turned with a beaming face towards Him. He, in truth, is numbered with the learned. The inmates of Paradise seek the blessing of his breath, and his lamp sheddeth its radiance over all who are in heaven and on earth. He, verily, is numbered with the inheritors of the Prophets. He that beholdeth him hath, verily, beheld the True One, and he that turneth towards him hath, verily, turned towards God, the Almighty, the All-Wise.

88

89    O ye the dawning-places of knowledge! Beware that ye
suffer not yourselves to become changed, for as ye change,
most men will, likewise, change. This, verily, is an injustice
unto yourselves and unto others. Unto this beareth witness
every man of discernment and insight. Ye are even as a
spring. If it be changed, so will the streams that branch out
from it be changed. Fear God, and be numbered with the
godly. In like manner, if the heart of man be corrupted, his
limbs will also be corrupted. And similarly, if the root of
a tree be corrupted, its branches, and its offshoots, and its
leaves, and its fruits, will be corrupted. Thus have We set
forth similitudes for your instruction, that perchance ye may
not be debarred by the things ye possess from attaining unto
that which hath been destined for you by Him Who is the
All-Glorious, the Most Bountiful.

90    It is indeed in Our power to take up a handful of dust and
to adorn it with the vesture of Our Names. This, however,
would be but a sign of Our favor, and not an indication of
any merit it may have inherently possessed. Thus hath it
been revealed in truth by Him Who is the Sovereign Revealer, the All-Knowing. Consider the Black Stone,[9] which God
hath made a point whereunto all men turn in adoration.
Hath this bounty been conferred upon it by virtue of its
innate excellence? Nay, by Mine own Self! Or doth such
distinction stem from its intrinsic worth? Nay, by Mine own
Being, Whose Essence all creation hath failed to grasp!

91    Again, consider the Mosque of Aqṣá and the other places
which We have made sanctuaries unto the people in every
land and region. The honor and distinction they enjoy is in
no wise due to their own merit, but stemmeth from their
relation to Our Manifestations, Whom We have appointed

as the Daysprings of Our Revelation amidst mankind, if ye be of them that understand. In this there lieth a wisdom inscrutable to all save God. Inquire, that He may graciously make plain unto you His purpose. His knowledge, verily, embraceth all things. Detach yourselves, O people, from the world and all its vanities, and heed not the call of such as have disbelieved in God and joined partners with Him. Arise above the horizon of utterance to extol and praise your Lord, the All-Merciful. This is that which God hath purposed for you; well is it with them who perceive it.

Say: O people! We have commanded you in Our Tablets    92
to strive, at the time of the promised Revelation, to sanctify your souls from all names, and to purify them from all that hath been created in the heavens or on the earth, that therein may appear the splendors of the Sun of Truth which shineth forth above the horizon of the Will of your Lord, the Almighty, the Most Great. We have, moreover, commanded you to cleanse your hearts from every trace of the love or hate of the peoples of the world, lest aught should divert you from one course or impel you towards another. This, verily, is among the weightiest counsels I have vouchsafed unto you in the perspicuous Book, for whoso attacheth himself to either of these shall be prevented from attaining a proper understanding of Our Cause. To this beareth witness every just and discerning soul.

Ye, however, have broken the Covenant of God, forgotten    93
His Testament, and at last turned away from Him Whose appearance hath solaced the eyes of every true believer in the Divine Unity. Lift up the veils and coverings that obscure your vision, and consider the testimonies of the Prophets and Messengers, that haply ye may recognize the Cause of

God in these days when the Promised One hath come invested with a mighty sovereignty. Fear God, and debar yourselves not from Him Who is the Dayspring of His signs. This shall, in truth, but profit your own selves; as to your Lord, He, verily, can afford to dispense with all creatures. From everlasting was He alone; there was none else besides Him. He it is in Whose name the standard of Divine Unity hath been planted upon the Sinai of the visible and invisible worlds, proclaiming that there is none other God but Me, the Peerless, the Glorious, the Incomparable.

94      Behold, however, how those who are but a creation of His Will and Command have turned aside from Him and have taken unto themselves a lord and master beside God; these, truly, are of the wayward. The mention of the All-Merciful hath at all times been upon their lips, and yet when He was manifested unto them through the power of truth they warred against Him. Wretched indeed shall be the plight of such as have broken the Covenant of their Lord when the Luminary of the world shone forth above the horizon of the Will of God, the Most Holy, the All-Knowing, the All-Wise! It was against God that they unsheathed the swords of malice and hatred, and yet they perceive it not. Methinks they remain dead and buried in the tombs of their selfish desires, though the breeze of God hath blown over all regions. They, truly, are wrapt in a dense and grievous veil. And oft as the verses of God are rehearsed unto them, they persist in proud disdain; it is as though they were devoid of all understanding, or had never heard the Melody of God, the Most Exalted, the All-Knowing.

95      Say: Alas for you! How can ye profess yourselves believers, when ye deny the verses of God, the Almighty, the

All-Knowing? Say: O people! Turn your faces unto your Lord, the All-Merciful. Beware lest ye be veiled by aught that hath been revealed in the Bayán: It was, in truth, revealed for no other purpose than to make mention of Me, the All-Powerful, the Most High, and had no other object than My Beauty. The whole world hath been filled with My testimony, if ye be of them that judge with fairness.

Had the Primal Point been someone else beside Me as ye   96 claim, and had attained My presence, verily He would have never allowed Himself to be separated from Me, but rather We would have had mutual delights with each other in My Days. He, in truth, wept sore in His remoteness from Me. He preceded Me that He might summon the people unto My Kingdom, as it hath been set forth in the Tablets, could ye but perceive it! O would that men of hearing might be found who could hear the voice of His lamentation in the Bayán bewailing that which hath befallen Me at the hands of these heedless souls, bemoaning His separation from Me and giving utterance to His longing to be united with Me, the Mighty, the Peerless. He, verily, beholdeth at this moment His Best-Beloved amidst those who were created to attain His Day and to prostrate themselves before Him, and yet who have inflicted in their tyranny such abasement upon Him as the pen confesseth its inability to describe.

Say: O people! We, verily, summoned you, in Our former   97 Revelation, unto this Scene of transcendent glory, this Seat of stainless sanctity, and announced unto you the advent of the Days of God. Yet, when the most great veil was rent asunder, and the Ancient Beauty came unto you in the clouds of God's decree, ye repudiated Him in Whom ye had believed aforetime. Woe betide you, O company of infidels!

Fear ye God, and nullify not the truth with the things ye possess. When the luminary of divine verses dawneth upon you from the horizon of the Pen of the King of all names and attributes, fall ye prostrate upon your faces before God, the Lord of the Worlds. For to bow down in adoration at the threshold of His door is indeed better for you than the worship of both worlds, and to submit to His Revelation is more profitable unto you than whatsoever hath been created in the heavens and on the earth.

98    Say: O people! I admonish you wholly for the sake of God, and seek no reward from you. For My recompense shall be with God, He Who hath brought Me into being, raised Me up by the power of truth, and made Me the Source of His remembrance amidst His creatures. Hasten to behold this divine and glorious Vision, the Spot wherein God hath established His Seat. Follow not that which the Evil One whispereth in your hearts, for he, verily, doth prompt you to walk after your lusts and covetous desires, and hindereth you from treading the straight Path which this all-embracing and all-compelling Cause hath opened.

99    Say: The Evil One hath appeared in such wise as the eye of creation hath never beheld. He Who is the Beauty of the All-Merciful hath likewise been made manifest with an adorning the like of which hath never been witnessed in the past. The Call of the All-Merciful hath been raised, and behind it the call of Satan. Well is it with them who hearken unto the Voice of God, and turn their faces towards His throne to behold a most holy and blessed Vision. For whoso cherisheth in his heart the love of anyone beside Me, be it to the extent of a grain of mustard seed, shall be unable to gain admittance into My Kingdom. To this beareth witness

that which adorneth the preamble of the Book of Existence, could ye but perceive it. Say: This is the Day whereon God's most great favor hath been made manifest. The voice of all who are in the heavens above and on the earth below proclaimeth My Name, and singeth forth My praises, could ye but hear it!

O Temple of Divine Revelation! Sound the trumpet in My Name! O Temple of Divine mysteries! Raise the clarion call of Thy Lord, the Unconditioned, the Unconstrained! O Maid of Heaven! Step forth from the chambers of Paradise and announce unto the people of the world: By the righteousness of God! He Who is the Best-Beloved of the worlds—He Who hath ever been the Desire of every perceiving heart, the Object of the adoration of all that are in heaven and on earth, and the Cynosure of the former and the latter generations—is now come! 100

Take heed lest ye hesitate in recognizing this resplendent Beauty when once He hath appeared in the plenitude of His sovereign might and majesty. He, verily, is the True One, and all else besides Him is as naught before a single one of His servants, and paleth into nothingness when brought face to face with the revelation of His splendors. Hasten, then, to attain the living waters of His grace, and be not of the negligent. As to him who hesitateth, though it be for less than a moment, God shall verily bring his works to naught and return him to the seat of wrath; wretched indeed is the abode of them that tarry! 101

## Pope Pius IX

O Pope! Rend the veils asunder. He Who is the Lord of Lords is come overshadowed with clouds, and the decree 102

45

hath been fulfilled by God, the Almighty, the Unrestrained. Dispel the mists through the power of thy Lord, and ascend unto the Kingdom of His names and attributes. Thus hath the Pen of the Most High commanded thee at the behest of thy Lord, the Almighty, the All-Compelling. He, verily, hath again come down from Heaven even as He came down from it the first time. Beware that thou dispute not with Him even as the Pharisees disputed with Him without a clear token or proof. On His right hand flow the living waters of grace, and on His left the choice Wine of justice, whilst before Him march the angels of Paradise, bearing the banners of His signs. Beware lest any name debar thee from God, the Creator of earth and heaven. Leave thou the world behind thee, and turn towards thy Lord, through Whom the whole earth hath been illumined.

103    We have adorned the Kingdom with the ornament of Our name, the All-Glorious. Thus hath it been decreed by God, the Fashioner of all things. Take heed lest thy vain imaginings withhold thee, when once the Sun of Certitude hath shone forth above the horizon of the Utterance of thy Lord, the Mighty, the Beneficent. Dwellest thou in palaces whilst He Who is the King of Revelation liveth in the most desolate of abodes? Leave them unto such as desire them, and set thy face with joy and delight towards the Kingdom.

104    Say: O peoples of the earth! Destroy the abodes of negligence with the hands of power and assurance, and raise up the mansions of true knowledge within your hearts, that the All-Merciful may shed the radiance of His light upon them. Better is this for you than all whereon the sun shineth, and unto this beareth witness He Who holdeth within His grasp the ultimate decree. The Breeze of God hath been wafted

over the world at the advent of the Desired One in His great glory, whereupon every stone and clod of earth hath cried out: "The Promised One is come! The Kingdom is God's, the Mighty, the Gracious, the Forgiving."

Beware lest human learning debar thee from Him Who is the Supreme Object of all knowledge, or lest the world deter thee from the One Who created it and set it upon its course. Arise in the name of thy Lord, the God of Mercy, amidst the peoples of the earth, and seize thou the Cup of Life with the hands of confidence. First drink thou therefrom, and proffer it then to such as turn towards it amongst the peoples of all faiths. Thus hath the Moon of Utterance risen above the horizon of wisdom and understanding. 105

Tear asunder the veils of human learning lest they hinder thee from Him Who is My name, the Self-Subsisting. Call thou to remembrance Him Who was the Spirit, Who, when He came, the most learned of His age pronounced judgment against Him in His own country, whilst he who was only a fisherman believed in Him. Take heed, then, ye men of understanding heart! Thou, in truth, art one of the suns of the heaven of His names. Guard thyself, lest darkness spread its veils over thee, and fold thee away from His light. Ponder, then, that which hath been sent down in the Book by thy Lord, the Almighty, the All-Bountiful. 106

Say: Still your pens, O concourse of divines, for lo, the shrill voice of the Pen of Glory hath been lifted up between earth and heaven. Cast away all that ye possess and take fast hold of that which We have revealed unto you with power and authority. The Hour that was concealed within the knowledge of God hath struck, whereupon all the atoms of the earth have proclaimed: "The Ancient of Days is come in 107

His great glory! Hasten unto Him, O peoples of the earth, with humble and contrite hearts." Say: We, in truth, have given Ourself as a ransom for your own lives. Alas, when We came once again, We beheld you fleeing from Us, whereat the eye of My loving-kindness wept sore over My people. Fear God, O ye that perceive.

108 Consider those who opposed the Son, when He came unto them with sovereignty and power. How many the Pharisees who were waiting to behold Him, and were lamenting over their separation from Him! And yet, when the fragrance of His coming was wafted over them, and His beauty was unveiled, they turned aside from Him and disputed with Him. Thus do We impart unto thee that which hath been recorded in the Books and Scriptures. None save a very few, who were destitute of any power amongst men, turned towards His face. And yet today every man endowed with power and invested with sovereignty prideth himself on His Name! In like manner, consider how numerous, in these days, are the monks who, in My Name, have secluded themselves in their churches, and who, when the appointed time was fulfilled, and We unveiled Our beauty, knew Us not, though they call upon Me at eventide and at dawn. We behold them clinging to My name, yet veiled from My Self. This, verily, is a strange thing.

109 Say: Take heed lest your devotions withhold you from Him Who is the object of all devotion, or your worship debar you from Him Who is the object of all worship. Rend asunder the veils of your idle fancies! This is your Lord, the Almighty, the All-Knowing, Who hath come to quicken the world and unite all who dwell on earth. Turn unto the Dayspring of Revelation, O people, and tarry not, be it for less

than the twinkling of an eye. Read ye the Evangel and yet refuse to acknowledge the All-Glorious Lord? This indeed beseemeth you not, O concourse of learned men!

Say: If ye deny this Revelation, by what proof have ye    110 believed in God? Produce it then. Thus hath the summons of God been sent down by the Pen of the Most High at the bidding of your Lord, the Most Glorious, in this Tablet from whose horizon the splendor of His Light hath shone forth. How many are My servants whose deeds have become veils between them and their own selves, and who have been kept back thereby from drawing nigh unto God, He Who causeth the winds to blow.

O concourse of monks! The fragrances of the All-Merciful    111 have wafted over all creation. Happy the man that hath forsaken his desires, and taken fast hold of guidance. He, indeed, is of those who have attained unto the presence of God in this Day, a Day whereon commotions have seized the dwellers of the earth and filled with dismay all save those who have been exempted by God, He Who layeth low the necks of men.

Adorn ye your bodies whilst the raiment of God is stained    112 with the blood of hatred at the hands of the people of denial? Issue forth from your habitations and bid the people enter the Kingdom of God, the Lord of the Day of Judgment. The Word which the Son concealed is made manifest. It hath been sent down in the form of the human temple in this day. Blessed be the Lord Who is the Father! He, verily, is come unto the nations in His most great majesty. Turn your faces towards Him, O concourse of the righteous!

O followers of all religions! We behold you wandering    113 distraught in the wilderness of error. Ye are the fish of this Ocean; wherefore do ye withhold yourselves from that which sustaineth you? Lo, it surgeth before your faces. Hasten unto it from every clime. This is the day whereon the Rock* crieth out and shouteth, and celebrateth the praise of its Lord, the All-Possessing, the Most High, saying: "Lo! The Father is come, and that which ye were promised in the Kingdom is fulfilled!" This is the Word which was preserved behind the veils of grandeur, and which, when the Promise came to pass, shed its radiance from the horizon of the Divine Will with clear tokens.

114 My body hath borne imprisonment that your souls may be released from bondage, and We have consented to be abased that ye may be exalted. Follow the Lord of glory and dominion, and not every ungodly oppressor. My body longeth for the cross, and Mine head awaiteth the thrust of the spear, in the path of the All-Merciful, that the world may be purged from its transgressions. Thus hath the Daystar of divine authority shone forth from the horizon of the Revelation of Him Who is the Possessor of all names and attributes.

115 The people of the Qur'án have risen against Us, and tormented Us with such a torment that the Holy Spirit lamented, and the thunder roared out, and the clouds wept over Us. Among the faithless is he who hath imagined that calamities can deter Bahá from fulfilling that which God, the Creator of all things, hath purposed. Say: Nay, by Him Who causeth the rain to fall! Nothing whatsoever can withhold Him from the remembrance of His Lord.

116 By the righteousness of God! Should they cast Him into a fire kindled on the continent, He will assuredly rear His

* Peter.

head in the midmost heart of the ocean and proclaim: "He is the Lord of all that are in heaven and all that are on earth!" And if they cast Him into a darksome pit, they will find Him seated on earth's loftiest heights calling aloud to all mankind: "Lo, the Desire of the World is come in His majesty, His sovereignty, His transcendent dominion!" And if He be buried beneath the depths of the earth, His Spirit soaring to the apex of heaven shall peal the summons: "Behold ye the coming of the Glory; witness ye the Kingdom of God, the Most Holy, the Gracious, the All-Powerful!" And if they shed His blood, every drop thereof shall cry out and invoke God in this Name through which the fragrance of His raiment hath been diffused in all directions.

Though threatened by the swords of Our enemies, We 117 summon all mankind unto God, the Fashioner of earth and heaven, and We render Him such aid as can be hindered by neither the hosts of tyranny nor the ascendancy of the people of iniquity. Say: O peoples of the earth! Scatter the idols of your vain imaginings in the name of your Lord, the All-Glorious, the All-Knowing, and turn ye unto Him in this Day which God hath made the King of days.

O Supreme Pontiff! Incline thine ear unto that which the 118 Fashioner of moldering bones counseleth thee, as voiced by Him Who is His Most Great Name. Sell all the embellished ornaments thou dost possess, and expend them in the path of God, Who causeth the night to return upon the day, and the day to return upon the night. Abandon thy kingdom unto the kings, and emerge from thy habitation, with thy face set towards the Kingdom, and, detached from the world, then speak forth the praises of thy Lord betwixt earth and heaven. Thus hath bidden thee He Who is the

Possessor of Names, on the part of thy Lord, the Almighty, the All-Knowing. Exhort thou the kings and say: "Deal equitably with men. Beware lest ye transgress the bounds fixed in the Book." This indeed becometh thee. Beware lest thou appropriate unto thyself the things of the world and the riches thereof. Leave them unto such as desire them, and cleave unto that which hath been enjoined upon thee by Him Who is the Lord of creation. Should anyone offer thee all the treasures of the earth, refuse to even glance upon them. Be as thy Lord hath been. Thus hath the Tongue of Revelation spoken that which God hath made the ornament of the book of creation.

119     Consider a pearl which shineth by virtue of its inherent nature. If it be covered with silk, its luster and beauty will be concealed. Likewise, man's distinction lieth in the excellence of his conduct and in the pursuit of that which beseemeth his station, not in childish play and pastimes. Know that thy true adornment consisteth in the love of God and in thy detachment from all save Him, and not in the luxuries thou dost possess. Abandon them unto those who seek after them and turn unto God, He Who causeth the rivers to flow.

120     Whatever proceeded from the tongue of the Son was revealed in parables, whilst He Who proclaimeth the Truth in this Day speaketh without them. Take heed lest thou cling to the cord of idle fancy and withhold thyself from that which hath been ordained in the Kingdom of God, the Almighty, the All-Bountiful. Should the inebriation of the wine of My verses seize thee, and thou determinest to present thyself before the throne of thy Lord, the Creator of earth and heaven, make My love thy vesture, and thy shield

remembrance of Me, and thy provision reliance upon God, the Revealer of all power.

O followers of the Son! We have once again sent John 121 unto you, and He, verily, hath cried out in the wilderness of the Bayán: O peoples of the world! Cleanse your eyes! The Day whereon ye can behold the Promised One and attain unto Him hath drawn nigh! O followers of the Gospel! Prepare the way! The Day of the advent of the Glorious Lord is at hand! Make ready to enter the Kingdom. Thus hath it been ordained by God, He Who causeth the dawn to break.

Give ear unto that which the Dove of Eternity warbleth 122 upon the twigs of the Divine Lote-Tree: O followers of the Son! We sent forth him who was named John to baptize you with water, that your bodies might be cleansed for the appearance of the Messiah. He, in turn, purified you with the fire of love and the water of the spirit in anticipation of these Days whereon the All-Merciful hath purposed to cleanse you with the water of life at the hands of His loving providence. This is that peerless One foretold by Isaiah, and the Comforter concerning Whom the Spirit had covenanted with you. Open your eyes, O concourse of bishops, that ye may behold your Lord seated upon the Throne of might and glory.

Say: O peoples of all faiths! Walk not in the ways of them 123 that followed the Pharisees and thus veiled themselves from the Spirit. They truly have strayed and are in error. The Ancient Beauty is come in His Most Great Name, and He wisheth to admit all mankind into His most holy Kingdom. The pure in heart behold the Kingdom of God manifest before His Face. Make haste thereunto and follow not the infidel and the ungodly. Should your eye be opposed thereto, pluck it out.[10] Thus hath it been decreed by the Pen of the Ancient of Days, as bidden by Him Who is the Lord of the entire creation. He, verily, hath come again that ye might be redeemed, O peoples of the earth. Will ye slay Him Who desireth to grant you eternal life? Fear God, O ye who are endued with insight.

124    O people! Hearken unto that which hath been revealed by your All-Glorious Lord, and turn your faces unto God, the Lord of this world and of the world to come. Thus doth He Who is the Dawning-Place of the Daystar of divine inspiration command you as bidden by the Fashioner of all mankind. We, verily, have created you for the light, and desire not to abandon you unto the fire. Come forth, O people, from darkness by the grace of this Sun which hath shone forth above the horizon of divine providence, and turn thereunto with sanctified hearts and assured souls, with seeing eyes and beaming faces. Thus counseleth you the Supreme Ordainer from the scene of His transcendent glory, that perchance His summons may draw you nigh unto the Kingdom of His names.

125    Blessed the one who hath remained faithful to the Covenant of God, and woe betide him who hath broken it and disbelieved in Him, the Knower of secrets. Say: This is the Day of Bounty! Bestir yourselves that I may make you monarchs in the realms of My Kingdom. If ye follow Me, ye shall behold that which ye were promised, and I will make you My companions in the dominion of My majesty and the intimates of My beauty in the heaven of My power forevermore. If ye rebel against Me, I will in My clemency endure

it patiently, that haply ye may awaken and rise up from the couch of heedlessness. Thus hath My mercy encompassed you. Fear ye God and follow not in the ways of those who have turned away from His face, though they invoke His name in the daytime and in the night season.

Verily, the day of ingathering is come, and all things have been separated from each other. He hath stored away that which He chose in the vessels of justice, and cast into fire that which befitteth it. Thus hath it been decreed by your Lord, the Mighty, the Loving, in this promised Day. He, verily, ordaineth what He pleaseth. There is none other God save He, the Almighty, the All-Compelling. The desire of the Divine Sifter hath been to store up every good thing for Mine own Self. Naught hath He spoken save to acquaint you with My Cause and to guide you to the path of Him whose mention hath adorned all the sacred Books. 126

Say: O concourse of Christians! We have, on a previous occasion, revealed Ourself unto you, and ye recognized Me not. This is yet another occasion vouchsafed unto you. This is the Day of God; turn ye unto Him. He, verily, hath come down from heaven even as He came down the first time, and He desireth to shelter you beneath the shade of His mercy. He, verily, is the Exalted, the Mighty, the Supreme Helper. The Beloved One loveth not that ye be consumed with the fire of your desires. Were ye to be shut out as by a veil from Him, this would be for no other reason than your own waywardness and ignorance. Ye make mention of Me, and know Me not. Ye call upon Me, and are heedless of My Revelation, notwithstanding that I came unto you from the heaven of pre-existence with surpassing glory. Rend the veils 127

55

THE SUMMONS OF THE LORD OF HOSTS

asunder in My name and through the power of My sovereignty that ye may discover a path unto your Lord.

128      The King of Glory proclaimeth from the tabernacle of majesty and grandeur His call, saying: O people of the Gospel! They who were not in the Kingdom have now entered it, whilst We behold you, in this day, tarrying at the gate. Rend the veils asunder by the power of your Lord, the Almighty, the All-Bounteous, and enter, then, in My name My Kingdom. Thus biddeth you He Who desireth for you everlasting life. He, verily, is potent over all things. Blessed are those who have recognized the Light and hastened unto it. They, verily, dwell in the Kingdom, and partake of the food and drink of God's chosen ones.

129      We behold you, O children of the Kingdom, in darkness. This, verily, beseemeth you not. Are ye, in the face of the Light, fearful because of your deeds? Direct yourselves towards Him. Your All-Glorious Lord hath blessed His lands with His footsteps. Thus do We make plain unto you the path of Him Whom the Spirit prophesied. I, verily, bear witness unto Him, even as He hath borne witness unto Me. Verily, He said: "Come ye after Me, and I will make you to become fishers of men." In this day, however, We say: "Come ye after Me, that We may make you to become the quickeners of mankind." Thus hath the decree been inscribed in this Tablet by the Pen of Revelation.

130      O Pen of the Most High! Bestir Thyself in remembrance of other kings in this blessed and luminous Book, that perchance they may rise from the couch of heedlessness and give ear unto that which the Nightingale singeth upon the branches of the Divine Lote-Tree, and hasten towards God in this most wondrous and sublime Revelation.

## Napoleon III

O King of Paris![11] Tell the priests to ring the bells no lon-   131
ger. By God, the True One! The Most Mighty Bell hath
appeared in the form of Him Who is the Most Great Name,
and the fingers of the Will of Thy Lord, the Most Exalted,
the Most High, toll it out in the heaven of Immortality in
His name, the All-Glorious. Thus have the mighty verses of
Thy Lord been again sent down unto thee, that thou mayest
arise to remember God, the Creator of earth and heaven, in
these days when all the tribes of the earth have mourned,
and the foundations of the cities have trembled, and the
dust of irreligion hath enwrapped all men, except such as
God, the All-Knowing, the All-Wise, was pleased to spare.
Say: He Who is the Unconstrained is come, in the clouds
of light, that He may quicken the world with the breezes
of His name, the Most Merciful, and unite its peoples, and
gather all men around this Table which hath been sent down
from heaven. Beware that ye deny not the favor of God after it hath been sent down unto you. Better is this for you
than that which ye possess; for that which is yours perisheth,
whilst that which is with God endureth. He, in truth, ordaineth what He pleaseth. Verily, the breezes of forgiveness
have been wafted from the direction of your Lord, the God
of Mercy; whoso turneth thereunto shall be cleansed of his
sins, and of all pain and sickness. Happy the man that hath
turned towards them, and woe betide him that hath turned
aside.

Wert thou to incline thine inner ear unto all created   132
things, thou wouldst hear: "The Ancient of Days is come
in His great glory!" Everything celebrateth the praise of its
Lord. Some have known God and remember Him; others

remember Him, yet know Him not. Thus have We set down Our decree in a perspicuous Tablet.

133    Give ear, O King, unto the Voice that calleth from the Fire which burneth in this verdant Tree, on this Sinai which hath been raised above the hallowed and snow-white Spot, beyond the Everlasting City; "Verily, there is none other God but Me, the Ever-Forgiving, the Most Merciful!" We, in truth, have sent Him Whom We aided with the Holy Spirit that He may announce unto you this Light that hath shone forth from the horizon of the Will of your Lord, the Most Exalted, the All-Glorious, and Whose signs have been revealed in the West. Set your faces towards Him on this Day which God hath exalted above all other days, and whereon the All-Merciful hath shed the splendor of His effulgent glory upon all who are in heaven and all who are on earth. Arise thou to serve God and help His Cause. He, verily, will assist thee with the hosts of the seen and unseen, and will set thee king over all that whereon the sun riseth. Thy Lord, in truth, is the All-Powerful, the Almighty.

134    The breezes of the Most Merciful have passed over all created things; happy the man that hath discovered their fragrance, and set himself towards them with a sound heart. Attire thy temple with the ornament of My Name, and thy tongue with remembrance of Me, and thine heart with love for Me, the Almighty, the Most High. We have desired for thee naught except that which is better for thee than what thou dost possess and all the treasures of the earth. Thy Lord, verily, is knowing, informed of all. Arise, in My Name, amongst My servants, and say: "O ye peoples of the earth! Turn yourselves towards Him Who hath turned towards you. He, verily, is the Face of God amongst you, and

His Testimony and His Guide unto you. He hath come to you with signs which none can produce." The voice of the Burning Bush is raised in the midmost heart of the world, and the Holy Spirit calleth aloud among the nations: "Lo, the Desired One is come with manifest dominion!"

O King! The stars of the heaven of knowledge have fallen, they who seek to establish the truth of My Cause through the things they possess, and who make mention of God in My Name. And yet, when I came unto them in My glory, they turned aside. They, indeed, are of the fallen. This is, truly, that which the Spirit of God hath announced, when He came with truth unto you, He with Whom the Jewish doctors disputed, till at last they perpetrated what hath made the Holy Spirit to lament, and the tears of them that have near access to God to flow. Consider how a Pharisee who had worshipped God for seventy years repudiated the Son when He appeared, whereas one who had committed adultery gained admittance into the Kingdom. Thus doth the Pen admonish thee as bidden by the Eternal King, that thou mayest be apprised of what came to pass aforetime and be reckoned in this day among them that truly believe. 135

Say: O concourse of monks! Seclude not yourselves in your churches and cloisters. Come ye out of them by My leave, and busy, then, yourselves with what will profit you and others. Thus commandeth you He Who is the Lord of the Day of Reckoning. Seclude yourselves in the stronghold of My love. This, truly, is the seclusion that befitteth you, could ye but know it. He that secludeth himself in his house is indeed as one dead. It behooveth man to show forth that which will benefit mankind. He that bringeth forth no fruit is fit for the fire. Thus admonisheth you your Lord; He, ver- 136 ily, is the Mighty, the Bountiful. Enter ye into wedlock, that after you another may arise in your stead. We, verily, have forbidden you lechery, and not that which is conducive to fidelity. Have ye clung unto the promptings of your nature, and cast behind your backs the statutes of God? Fear ye God, and be not of the foolish. But for man, who, on My earth, would remember Me, and how could My attributes and My names be revealed? Reflect, and be not of them that have shut themselves out as by a veil from Him, and were of those that are fast asleep. He that married not could find no place wherein to abide, nor where to lay His head, by reason of what the hands of the treacherous had wrought. His holiness consisted not in the things ye have believed and imagined, but rather in the things which belong unto Us. Ask, that ye may be made aware of His station which hath been exalted above the vain imaginings of all the peoples of the earth. Blessed are they that understand.

137  O King! We heard the words thou didst utter in answer to the Czar of Russia, concerning the decision made regarding the war.[12] Thy Lord, verily, knoweth, is informed of all. Thou didst say: "I lay asleep upon my couch, when the cry of the oppressed, who were drowned in the Black Sea, wakened me." This is what We heard thee say, and, verily, thy Lord is witness unto what I say. We testify that that which wakened thee was not their cry but the promptings of thine own passions, for We tested thee, and found thee wanting. Comprehend the meaning of My words, and be thou of the discerning. It is not Our wish to address thee words of condemnation, out of regard for the dignity We conferred upon thee in this mortal life. We, verily, have chosen courtesy, and made it the true mark of such as are nigh unto Him. Courtesy is, in truth, a raiment which fitteth all men, whether

young or old. Well is it with him that adorneth his temple therewith, and woe unto him who is deprived of this great bounty. Hadst thou been sincere in thy words, thou wouldst have not cast behind thy back the Book of God, when it was sent unto thee by Him Who is the Almighty, the All-Wise. We have proved thee through it, and found thee other than that which thou didst profess. Arise, and make amends for that which escaped thee. Erelong the world and all that thou possessest will perish, and the kingdom will remain unto God, thy Lord and the Lord of thy fathers of old. It behooveth thee not to conduct thine affairs according to the dictates of thy desires. Fear the sighs of this Wronged One, and shield Him from the darts of such as act unjustly.

For what thou hast done, thy kingdom shall be thrown into confusion, and thine empire shall pass from thine hands, as a punishment for that which thou hast wrought.[13] Then wilt thou know how thou hast plainly erred. Commotions shall seize all the people in that land, unless thou arisest to help this Cause, and followest Him Who is the Spirit of God in this, the Straight Path. Hath thy pomp made thee proud? By My Life! It shall not endure; nay, it shall soon pass away, unless thou holdest fast by this firm Cord. We see abasement hastening after thee, whilst thou art of those who are fast asleep. It behooveth thee when thou hearest His Voice calling from the seat of glory to cast away all that thou possessest, and cry out: "Here am I, O Lord of all that is in heaven and all that is on earth!"

O King! We were in 'Iráq, when the hour of parting arrived. At the bidding of the King of Islám* We set Our steps in his direction. Upon Our arrival, there befell Us at the

138

139

* The Sultán of Turkey.

hands of the malicious that which the books of the world can never adequately recount. Thereupon the inmates of Paradise, and they that dwell within the retreats of holiness, lamented; and yet the people are wrapped in a thick veil! Say: Do ye cavil at Him Who hath come unto you bearing the clear evidence of God and His proof, the testimony of God and His signs? These things are not from Himself; nay, rather they proceed from the One Who hath raised Him up, sent Him forth through the power of truth, and made Him to be a lamp unto all mankind.

140    More grievous became Our plight from day to day, nay, from hour to hour, until they took Us forth from Our prison and made Us, with glaring injustice, enter the Most Great Prison. And if anyone ask them: "For what crime were they imprisoned?," they would answer and say: "They, verily, sought to supplant the Faith with a new religion!" If that which is ancient be what ye prefer, wherefore, then, have ye discarded that which hath been set down in the Torah and the Evangel? Clear it up, O men! By My life! There is no place for you to flee to in this day. If this be My crime, then Muḥammad, the Apostle of God, committed it before Me, and before Him He Who was the Spirit of God, and yet earlier He Who conversed with God. And if My sin be this, that I have exalted the Word of God and revealed His Cause, then indeed am I the greatest of sinners! Such a sin I will not barter for the kingdoms of earth and heaven.

141    Upon Our arrival at this Prison, We purposed to transmit to the kings the messages of their Lord, the Mighty, the All-Praised. Though We have transmitted to them, in several Tablets, that which We were commanded, yet We do it once again as a token of God's grace. Perchance they

may recognize the Lord, Who hath come down in the clouds with manifest sovereignty.

As My tribulations multiplied, so did My love for God 142 and for His Cause increase, in such wise that all that befell Me from the hosts of the wayward was powerless to deter Me from My purpose. Should they hide Me away in the depths of the earth, yet would they find Me riding aloft on the clouds, and calling out unto God, the Lord of strength and of might. I have offered Myself up in the way of God, and I yearn after tribulations in My love for Him, and for the sake of His good pleasure. Unto this bear witness the woes which now afflict Me, the like of which no other man hath suffered. Every single hair of Mine head calleth out that which the Burning Bush uttered on Sinai, and each vein of My body invoketh God and saith: "O would I had been severed in Thy path, so that the world might be quickened, and all its peoples be united!" Thus hath it been decreed by Him Who is the All-Knowing, the All-Informed.

Know of a truth that your subjects are God's trust amongst 143 you. Watch ye, therefore, over them as ye watch over your own selves. Beware that ye allow not wolves to become the shepherds of the fold, or pride and conceit to deter you from turning unto the poor and the desolate. Wert thou to quaff the mystic Wine of everlasting life from the chalice of the words of thy Lord, the All-Merciful, thou wouldst be enabled to forsake all that thou dost possess and to proclaim My Name before all mankind. Cleanse then thy soul with the waters of detachment. Verily, this is the Remembrance that hath shone forth above the horizon of creation, which shall purge thy soul from the dross of the world. Abandon thy palaces to the people of the graves, and thine empire to whosoever desireth it, and turn, then, unto the Kingdom. This, verily, is what God hath chosen for thee, wert thou of them that turn unto Him. They that have failed to turn unto the Countenance of God in this Revelation are indeed bereft of life. They move as bidden by their own selfish desires, and are in truth accounted among the dead. Shouldst thou desire to bear the weight of thy dominion, bear it then to aid the Cause of thy Lord. Glorified be this station which whoever attaineth thereunto hath attained unto all good that proceedeth from Him Who is the All-Knowing, the All-Wise.

144 Arise thou, in My name, above the horizon of renunciation, and set, then, thy face towards the Kingdom, at the bidding of thy Lord, the Lord of strength and of might. Through the power of My sovereignty stand before the inhabitants of the world and say: "O people! The Day is come, and the fragrances of God have been wafted over the whole of creation. They that have turned away from His Face are the helpless victims of their corrupt inclinations. They are indeed of them that have gone astray."

145 Adorn the body of Thy kingdom with the raiment of My name, and arise, then, to teach My Cause. Better is this for thee than that which thou possessest. God will, thereby, exalt thy name among all the kings. Potent is He over all things. Walk thou amongst men in the name of God, and by the power of His might, that thou mayest show forth His signs amidst the peoples of the earth. Burn thou brightly with the flame of this undying Fire which the All-Merciful hath ignited in the midmost heart of creation, that through thee the heat of His love may be kindled within the hearts of His favored ones. Follow in My way and enrapture the

hearts of men through remembrance of Me, the Almighty, the Most Exalted.

Say: He from whom, in this day, the sweet savors of the remembrance of His Lord, the All-Merciful, have not been diffused, is indeed unworthy of the station of man. He, verily, is of them that have followed their own desires, and shall erelong find himself in grievous loss. Doth it behoove you to relate yourselves to Him Who is the God of mercy, and yet commit the things which the Evil One hath committed? Nay, by the Beauty of Him Who is the All-Glorified! could ye but know it. Purge your hearts from love of the world, and your tongues from calumny, and your limbs from whatsoever may withhold you from drawing nigh unto God, the Mighty, the All-Praised. Say: By the world is meant that which turneth you aside from Him Who is the Dawning-Place of Revelation, and inclineth you unto that which is unprofitable unto you. Verily, the thing that deterreth you, in this day, from God is worldliness in its essence. Eschew it, and approach the Most Sublime Vision, this shining and resplendent Seat. Blessed is he who alloweth nothing whatsoever to intervene between him and his Lord. No harm, assuredly, can befall him if he partaketh with justice of the benefits of this world, inasmuch as We have created all things for such of Our servants as truly believe in God.

Should your words, O people, be at variance with your deeds, what then shall distinguish you from those who profess their faith in the Lord, their God, and yet, when He came down to them overshadowed with clouds, rejected Him and waxed proud before God, the Incomparable, the Omniscient? Shed not the blood of anyone, O people, neither judge ye anyone unjustly. Thus have ye been com-

146

147

manded by Him Who knoweth, Who is informed of all. They that commit disorders in the land after it hath been well ordered, these indeed have outstepped the bounds that have been set in the Book. Wretched shall be the abode of the transgressors!

148    God hath prescribed unto everyone the duty of teaching His Cause. Whoever ariseth to discharge this duty, must needs, ere he proclaimeth His Message, adorn himself with the ornament of an upright and praiseworthy character, so that his words may attract the hearts of such as are receptive to his call. Without it, he can never hope to influence his hearers. Thus doth God instruct you. He, verily, is the Ever-Forgiving, the Most Compassionate.

149    They who exhort others unto justice, while themselves committing iniquity, stand accused of falsehood by the inmates of the Kingdom and by those who circle round the throne of their Lord, the Almighty, the Beneficent, for that which their tongues have uttered. Commit not, O people, that which dishonoreth your name and the fair name of the Cause of God amongst men. Beware lest ye approach that which your minds abhor. Fear God and follow not in the footsteps of them that are gone astray. Deal not treacherously with the substance of your neighbor. Be ye trustworthy on earth, and withhold not from the poor the things given unto you by God through His grace. He, verily, will bestow upon you the double of what ye possess. He, in truth, is the All-Bounteous, the Most Generous.

150    Say: We have ordained that our Cause be taught through the power of utterance. Beware lest ye dispute idly with anyone. Whoso ariseth wholly for the sake of his Lord to teach His Cause, the Holy Spirit shall strengthen him and inspire

him with that which will illumine the heart of the world, how much more the hearts of those who seek Him. O people of Bahá! Subdue the citadels of men's hearts with the swords of wisdom and of utterance. They that dispute, as prompted by their desires, are indeed wrapped in a palpable veil. Say: The sword of wisdom is hotter than summer heat, and sharper than blades of steel, if ye do but understand. Draw it forth in My name and through the power of My might, and conquer then with it the cities of the hearts of them that have secluded themselves in the stronghold of their corrupt desires. Thus biddeth you the Pen of the All-Glorious, whilst seated beneath the swords of the wayward.

If ye become aware of a sin committed by another, conceal it, that God may conceal your own sin. He, verily, is the Concealer, the Lord of grace abounding. O ye rich ones on earth! If ye encounter one who is poor, treat him not disdainfully. Reflect upon that whereof ye were created. Every one of you was created of a sorry germ.[14] It behooveth you to observe truthfulness, whereby your temples shall be adorned, your names uplifted, your stations exalted amidst men, and a mighty recompense assured for you before God.

Give ear, O peoples of the earth, unto that which the Pen of the Lord of all nations commandeth you. Know ye of a certainty that the Dispensations of the past have attained their highest, their final consummation in the Law that hath branched out from this Most Great Ocean. Haste ye thereunto at Our behest. We, verily, ordain as We please. Regard ye the world as a man's body, which is afflicted with divers ailments, and the recovery of which dependeth upon the harmonizing of all of its component elements. Gather ye

151

152

around that which We have prescribed unto you, and walk not in the ways of such as create dissension.

153      All feasts have attained their consummation in the two Most Great Festivals, and in two other Festivals that fall on the twin days—the first of the Most Great Festivals being those days whereon God shed the effulgent glory of His most excellent Names upon all who are in heaven and on earth, and the second being that day on which We raised up the One Who announced unto the people the glad-tidings of this Great Announcement.[15] Thus hath it been set down in the Book by Him Who is the Mighty, the Powerful. On other than these four consummate days, engage ye in your daily occupations, and withhold yourselves not from the pursuit of your trades and crafts. Thus hath the command been issued and the law gone forth from Him Who is your Lord, the All-Knowing, the All-Wise.

154      Say: O concourse of priests and monks! Eat ye of that which God hath made lawful unto you and do not shun meat. God hath, as a token of His grace, granted you leave to partake thereof save during a brief period. He, verily, is the Mighty, the Beneficent. Forsake all that ye possess and hold fast unto that which God hath purposed. This is that which profiteth you, if ye be of them that comprehend. We have ordained a fast of nineteen days in the most temperate of the seasons, and have in this resplendent and luminous Dispensation relieved you from more than this. Thus have We set forth and made clear unto you that which ye are bidden to observe, that ye may follow the commandments of God and be united in that which the Almighty, the All-Wise, hath appointed unto you. He Who is your Lord, the All-Merciful, cherisheth in His heart the desire of beholding the entire human race as one

soul and one body. Haste ye to win your share of God's good grace and mercy in this Day that eclipseth all other created Days. How great the felicity that awaiteth the man that forsaketh all he hath in a desire to obtain the things of God! Such a man, We testify, is among God's blessed ones.

O King! Bear thou witness unto that which God hath Himself and for Himself borne witness ere the creation of earth and heaven, that there is none other God but Me, the One, the Single, the Most Exalted, the Incomparable, the Inaccessible. Arise with the utmost steadfastness in the Cause of thy Lord, the All-Glorious. Thus hast thou been instructed in this wondrous Tablet. We, verily, have desired naught for thee save that which is better for thee than all that is on earth. Unto this testify all created things and beyond them this perspicuous Book. $\qquad$ 155

Meditate on the world and the state of its people. He, for Whose sake the world was called into being, hath been imprisoned in the most desolate of cities,* by reason of that which the hands of the wayward have wrought. From the horizon of His prison-city He summoneth mankind unto the Dayspring of God, the Exalted, the Great. Exultest thou over the treasures thou dost possess, knowing they shall perish? Rejoicest thou in that thou rulest a span of earth, when the whole world, in the estimation of the people of Bahá, is worth as much as the black in the eye of a dead ant? Abandon it unto such as have set their affections upon it, and turn thou unto Him Who is the Desire of the world. Whither are gone the proud and their palaces? Gaze thou into their tombs, that thou mayest profit by this example, $\qquad$ 156

---

* 'Akká.

inasmuch as We made it a lesson unto every beholder. Were the breezes of Revelation to seize thee, thou wouldst flee the world, and turn unto the Kingdom, and wouldst expend all thou possessest, that thou mayest draw nigh unto this sublime Vision.

157 We behold the generality of mankind worshipping names and exposing themselves, as thou dost witness, to dire perils in the mere hope of perpetuating their names, whilst every perceiving soul testifieth that after death one's name shall avail him nothing except insofar as it beareth a relationship unto God, the Almighty, the All-Praised. Thus have their vain imaginings taken hold of them in requital for that which their hands have wrought. Consider the pettiness of men's minds. They seek with utmost exertion that which profiteth them not, and yet wert thou to ask of them: "Is there any advantage in that which ye desire?," thou wouldst find them sorely perplexed. Were a fair-minded soul to be found, he would reply: "Nay, by the Lord of the worlds!" Such is the condition of the people and of that which they possess. Leave them in their folly and turn thy sight unto God. This is in truth that which beseemeth thee. Hearken then unto the counsel of thy Lord, and say: Lauded art Thou, O God of all who are in heaven and on earth!

## Czar Alexander II

158 O Czar of Russia! Incline thine ear unto the voice of God, the King, the Holy, and turn thou unto Paradise, the Spot wherein abideth He Who, among the Concourse on high, beareth the most excellent titles, and Who, in the kingdom of creation, is called by the name of God, the Effulgent, the All-Glorious. Beware lest thy desire deter thee from turning

towards the face of thy Lord, the Compassionate, the Most Merciful. We, verily, have heard the thing for which thou didst supplicate thy Lord, whilst secretly communing with Him. Wherefore, the breeze of My loving-kindness wafted forth, and the sea of My mercy surged, and We answered thee in truth. Thy Lord, verily, is the All-Knowing, the All-Wise. Whilst I lay chained and fettered in the prison, one of thy ministers extended Me his aid. Wherefore hath God ordained for thee a station which the knowledge of none can comprehend except His knowledge. Beware lest thou barter away this sublime station. Thy Lord, verily, doeth what He willeth. What He pleaseth will God abrogate or confirm, and with Him is the knowledge of all things in a Guarded Tablet.

Beware lest thy sovereignty withhold thee from Him Who is the Supreme Sovereign. He, verily, is come with His Kingdom, and all the atoms cry aloud: "Lo! The Lord is come in His great majesty!" He Who is the Father is come, and the Son, in the holy vale, crieth out: "Here am I, here am I, O Lord, My God!," whilst Sinai circleth round the House, and the Burning Bush calleth aloud: "The All-Bounteous is come mounted upon the clouds! Blessed is he that draweth nigh unto Him, and woe betide them that are far away." 159

Arise thou amongst men in the name of this all-compelling Cause, and summon, then, the nations unto God, the Exalted, the Great. Be thou not of them who called upon God by one of His names, but who, when He Who is the Object of all names appeared, denied Him and turned aside from Him, and, in the end, pronounced sentence against Him with manifest injustice. Consider and call thou to mind the days whereon the Spirit of God appeared, and Herod gave 160 judgment against Him. God, however, aided Him with the hosts of the unseen, and protected Him with truth, and sent Him down unto another land, according to His promise. He, verily, ordaineth what He pleaseth. Thy Lord truly preserveth whom He willeth, be he in the midst of the seas, or in the maw of the serpent, or beneath the sword of the oppressor.

161  Blessed be the king whom the veils of glory have not deterred from turning unto the Dayspring of beauty and who hath forsaken his all in his desire to obtain the things of God. He, indeed, is accounted in the sight of God as the most excellent of men, and is extolled by the inmates of Paradise and them that circle morn and eve round the Throne on high.

162  Again I say: Hearken unto My voice that calleth from My prison, that it may acquaint thee with the things that have befallen My Beauty, at the hands of them that are the manifestations of My glory, and that thou mayest perceive how great hath been My patience, notwithstanding My might, and how immense My forbearance, notwithstanding My power. By My life! Couldst thou but know the things sent down by My Pen, and discover the treasures of My Cause, and the pearls of My mysteries which lie hid in the seas of My names and in the goblets of My words, thou wouldst, in thy love for My name, and in thy longing for My glorious and sublime Kingdom, lay down thy life in My path. Know thou that though My body be beneath the swords of My foes, and My limbs be beset with incalculable afflictions, yet My spirit is filled with a gladness with which all the joys of the earth can never compare.

Set thine heart towards Him Who is the Point of adora-  163
tion for the world, and say: "O peoples of the earth! Have
ye denied the One in Whose path He Who came with the
truth, bearing the announcement of your Lord, the Exalted,
the Great, suffered martyrdom?" Say: This is an Announcement whereat the hearts of the Prophets and Messengers
have rejoiced. This is the One Whom the heart of the world
remembereth, and is promised in the Books of God, the
Mighty, the All-Wise. The hands of the Messengers were, in
their desire to meet Me, upraised towards God, the Mighty,
the Glorified. Unto this testifieth that which hath been sent
down in the sacred Scriptures by Him Who is the Lord of
might and power.

Some lamented in their separation from Me, others endured  164
hardships in My path, and still others laid down their lives for
the sake of My Beauty, could ye but know it. Say: I, verily, have
not sought to extol Mine own Self, but rather God Himself,
were ye to judge fairly. Naught can be seen in Me except God
and His Cause, could ye but perceive it. I am the One Whom
the tongue of Isaiah hath extolled, the One with Whose name
both the Torah and the Evangel were adorned. Thus hath it
been decreed in the Scriptures of thy Lord, the Most Merciful.
He, verily, hath borne witness unto Me, as I bear witness unto
Him. And God testifieth to the truth of My words.

Say: The Books have been sent down for naught but My  165
remembrance. Whosoever is receptive to their call shall perceive therefrom the sweet fragrances of My name and My
praise; and he who hath unstopped the ear of his inmost
heart shall hear from every word thereof: "The True One is
come! He indeed is the beloved of the worlds!"

166     It is for the sake of God alone that My tongue counseleth you and that My pen moveth to make mention of you, for neither can the malice and denial of all who dwell on earth harm Me, nor the allegiance of the entire creation profit Me. We, verily, exhort you unto that which We were commanded, and desire naught from you except that ye draw nigh unto what shall profit you in both this world and the world to come. Say: Will ye slay Him Who summoneth you unto life everlasting? Fear ye God, and follow not every contumacious oppressor.

167     O proud ones of the earth! Do ye believe yourselves to be abiding in palaces whilst He Who is the King of Revelation resideth in the most desolate of abodes? Nay, by My life! In tombs do ye dwell, could ye but perceive it. Verily, he who faileth, in these days, to be stirred by the breeze of God is accounted among the dead in the sight of Him Who is the Lord of all names and attributes. Arise, then, from the tombs of self and desire and turn unto the Kingdom of God, the Possessor of the Throne on high and of earth below, that ye may behold that which ye were promised aforetime by your Lord, the All-Knowing.

168     Think ye that the things ye possess shall profit you? Soon others will possess them and ye will return unto the dust with none to help or succor you. What advantage is there in a life that can be overtaken by death, or in an existence that is doomed to extinction, or in a prosperity that is subject to change? Cast away the things that ye possess and set your faces toward the favors of God which have been sent down in this wondrous Name.

169     Thus doth the Pen of the Most High warble unto thee its melodies by the leave of thy Lord, the All-Glorious. When

thou hast heard and recited them, say: "Praise be unto Thee, O Lord of all the worlds, inasmuch as Thou hast made mention of me through the tongue of Him Who is the Manifestation of Thy Self at a time when He was confined in the Most Great Prison, that the whole world might attain unto true liberty."

Blessed be the king whose sovereignty hath withheld him 170 not from his Sovereign, and who hath turned unto God with his heart. He, verily, is accounted of those that have attained unto that which God, the Mighty, the All-Wise, hath willed. Erelong will such a one find himself numbered with the monarchs of the realms of the Kingdom. Thy Lord is, in truth, potent over all things. He giveth what He willeth to whomsoever He willeth, and withholdeth what He pleaseth from whomsoever He willeth. He, verily, is the All-Powerful, the Almighty.

## Queen Victoria

O Queen in London! Incline thine ear unto the voice of 171 thy Lord, the Lord of all mankind, calling from the Divine Lote-Tree: Verily, no God is there but Me, the Almighty, the All-Wise! Cast away all that is on earth, and attire the head of thy kingdom with the crown of the remembrance of thy Lord, the All-Glorious. He, in truth, hath come unto the world in His most great glory, and all that hath been mentioned in the Gospel hath been fulfilled. The land of Syria hath been honored by the footsteps of its Lord, the Lord of all men, and north and south are both inebriated with the wine of His presence. Blessed is the man that hath inhaled the fragrance of the Most Merciful, and turned unto the Dawning-Place of His Beauty, in this resplendent Dawn.

The Mosque of Aqsá vibrateth through the breezes of its Lord, the All-Glorious, whilst Baṭhá* trembleth at the voice of God, the Exalted, the Most High. Whereupon every single stone of them celebrateth the praise of the Lord, through this Great Name.

172 Lay aside thy desire, and set then thine heart towards thy Lord, the Ancient of Days. We make mention of thee for the sake of God, and desire that thy name may be exalted through thy remembrance of God, the Creator of earth and heaven. He, verily, is witness unto that which I say. We have been informed that thou hast forbidden the trading in slaves, both men and women. This, verily, is what God hath enjoined in this wondrous Revelation. God hath, truly, destined a reward for thee, because of this. He, verily, will pay the doer of good his due recompense, wert thou to follow what hath been sent unto thee by Him Who is the All-Knowing, the All-Informed. As to him who turneth aside, and swelleth with pride, after the clear tokens have come unto him from the Revealer of signs, his work shall God bring to naught. He, in truth, hath power over all things. Man's actions are acceptable after his having recognized (the Manifestation). He that turneth aside from the True One is indeed the most veiled amongst His creatures. Thus hath it been decreed by Him Who is the Almighty, the Most Powerful.

173 We have also heard that thou hast entrusted the reins of counsel into the hands of the representatives of the people. Thou, indeed, hast done well, for thereby the foundations of the edifice of thine affairs will be strengthened, and the

---

* Mecca.

hearts of all that are beneath thy shadow, whether high or low, will be tranquillized. It behooveth them, however, to be trustworthy among His servants, and to regard themselves as the representatives of all that dwell on earth. This is what counseleth them, in this Tablet, He Who is the Ruler, the All-Wise. And if any one of them directeth himself towards the Assembly, let him turn his eyes unto the Supreme Horizon, and say: "O my God! I ask Thee, by Thy most glorious Name, to aid me in that which will cause the affairs of Thy servants to prosper, and Thy cities to flourish. Thou, indeed, hast power over all things!" Blessed is he that entereth the Assembly for the sake of God, and judgeth between men with pure justice. He, indeed, is of the blissful.

O ye the elected representatives of the people in every land! Take ye counsel together, and let your concern be only for that which profiteth mankind and bettereth the condition thereof, if ye be of them that scan heedfully. Regard the world as the human body which, though at its creation whole and perfect, hath been afflicted, through various causes, with grave disorders and maladies. Not for one day did it gain ease, nay its sickness waxed more severe, as it fell under the treatment of ignorant physicians, who gave full rein to their personal desires and have erred grievously. And if, at one time, through the care of an able physician, a member of that body was healed, the rest remained afflicted as before. Thus informeth you the All-Knowing, the All-Wise.

We behold it, in this day, at the mercy of rulers so drunk with pride that they cannot discern clearly their own best advantage, much less recognize a Revelation so bewildering and challenging as this. And whenever any one of them hath striven to improve its condition, his motive hath been his own gain, whether confessedly so or not; and the unworthiness of this motive hath limited his power to heal or cure.

176     That which the Lord hath ordained as the sovereign remedy and mightiest instrument for the healing of all the world is the union of all its peoples in one universal Cause, one common Faith. This can in no wise be achieved except through the power of a skilled, an all-powerful and inspired Physician. This, verily, is the truth, and all else naught but error. Each time that Most Mighty Instrument hath come, and that Light shone forth from the Ancient Dayspring, He was withheld by ignorant physicians who, even as clouds, interposed themselves between Him and the world. It failed, therefore, to recover, and its sickness hath persisted until this day. They indeed were powerless to protect it, or to effect a cure, whilst He Who hath been the Manifestation of Power amongst men was withheld from achieving His purpose, by reason of what the hands of the ignorant physicians have wrought.

177     Consider these days in which He Who is the Ancient Beauty hath come in the Most Great Name, that He may quicken the world and unite its peoples. They, however, rose up against Him with sharpened swords, and committed that which caused the Faithful Spirit to lament, until in the end they imprisoned Him in the most desolate of cities, and broke the grasp of the faithful upon the hem of His robe. Were anyone to tell them: "The World Reformer is come," they would answer and say: "Indeed it is proven that He is a fomenter of discord!," and this notwithstanding that they have never associated with Him, and have perceived that He did not seek, for one moment, to protect Himself. At all times He was at the mercy of the wicked doers. At one time they cast Him into prison, at another they banished Him,

and at yet another hurried Him from land to land. Thus have they pronounced judgment against Us, and God, truly, is aware of what I say. Such men are reckoned by God among the most ignorant of His creatures. They cut off their own limbs and perceive it not; they deprive themselves of that which is best for them, and know it not. They are even as a young child who can distinguish neither the mischief-maker from the reformer nor the wicked from the righteous. We behold them in this Day wrapt in a palpable veil.

O ye rulers of the earth! Wherefore have ye clouded the radiance of the Sun, and caused it to cease from shining? Hearken unto the counsel given you by the Pen of the Most High, that haply both ye and the poor may attain unto tranquility and peace. We beseech God to assist the kings of the earth to establish peace on earth. He, verily, doth what He willeth. 178

O kings of the earth! We see you increasing every year your expenditures, and laying the burden thereof on your subjects. This, verily, is wholly and grossly unjust. Fear the sighs and tears of this Wronged One, and lay not excessive burdens on your peoples. Do not rob them to rear palaces for yourselves; nay rather choose for them that which ye choose for yourselves. Thus We unfold to your eyes that which profiteth you, if ye but perceive. Your people are your treasures. Beware lest your rule violate the commandments of God, and ye deliver your wards to the hands of the robber. By them ye rule, by their means ye subsist, by their aid ye conquer. Yet, how disdainfully ye look upon them! How strange, how very strange! 179

Now that ye have refused the Most Great Peace, hold ye fast unto this, the Lesser Peace, that haply ye may in 180 some degree better your own condition and that of your dependents.

181    O rulers of the earth! Be reconciled among yourselves, that ye may need no more armaments save in a measure to safeguard your territories and dominions. Beware lest ye disregard the counsel of the All-Knowing, the Faithful.

182    Be united, O kings of the earth, for thereby will the tempest of discord be stilled amongst you, and your peoples find rest, if ye be of them that comprehend. Should any one among you take up arms against another, rise ye all against him, for this is naught but manifest justice. Thus did We exhort you in the Tablet sent down aforetime,* and We admonish you once again to follow that which hath been revealed by Him Who is the Almighty, the All-Wise. Should anyone seek refuge with you, extend unto him your protection and betray him not. Thus doth the Pen of the Most High counsel you, as bidden by Him Who is the All-Knowing, the All-Informed.

183    Beware lest ye act as did the King of Islám** when We came unto him at his bidding. His ministers pronounced judgment against Us with such injustice that all creation lamented and the hearts of those who are nigh unto God were consumed. The winds of self and passion move them as they will, and We found them all bereft of constancy. They are, indeed, of those that are far astray.

184    Rein in Thy pen, O Pen of the Ancient of Days, and leave them to themselves, for they are immersed in their idle

---

* The Súriy-i-Mulúk.
** The Sulṭán of Turkey.

fancies. Make Thou mention of the Queen, that she may turn with a pure heart unto the scene of transcendent glory, may withhold not her eyes from gazing toward her Lord, the Supreme Ordainer, and may become acquainted with that which hath been revealed in the Books and Tablets by the Creator of all mankind, He through Whom the sun hath been darkened and the moon eclipsed, and through Whom the Call hath been raised betwixt earth and heaven.

Turn thou unto God and say: O my Sovereign Lord! I am but a vassal of Thine, and Thou art, in truth, the King of kings. I have lifted my suppliant hands unto the heaven of Thy grace and Thy bounties. Send down, then, upon me from the clouds of Thy generosity that which will rid me of all save Thee, and draw me nigh unto Thyself. I beseech Thee, O my Lord, by Thy name, which Thou hast made the king of names and the manifestation of Thyself to all who are in heaven and on earth, to rend asunder the veils that have intervened between me and my recognition of the Dawning-Place of Thy signs and the Dayspring of Thy Revelation. Thou art, verily, the Almighty, the All-Powerful, the All-Bounteous. Deprive me not, O my Lord, of the fragrances of the Robe of Thy mercy in Thy days, and write down for me that which Thou hast written down for Thy handmaidens who have believed in Thee and in Thy signs, and have recognized Thee, and set their hearts towards the horizon of Thy Cause. Thou art truly the Lord of the worlds and of those who show mercy the Most Merciful. Assist me, then, O my God, to remember Thee amongst Thy handmaidens, and to aid Thy Cause in Thy lands. Accept, then, that which hath escaped me when the light of Thy countenance shone forth. Thou, indeed, hast power over all things.

185

Glory be to Thee, O Thou in Whose hand is the kingdom of the heavens and of the earth.

### Náṣiri'd-Dín Sháh

186   O King of the Earth! Hearken unto the call of this Vassal: Verily, I am a Servant Who hath believed in God and in His signs, and have sacrificed Myself in His path. Unto this bear witness the woes which now beset Me, woes the like of which no man hath ever before sustained. My Lord, the All-Knowing, testifieth to the truth of My words. I have summoned the people unto none save God, thy Lord and the Lord of the worlds, and have endured for love of Him such afflictions as the eye of creation hath never beheld. To this testify those whom the veils of human fancy have not deterred from turning unto the Most Sublime Vision, and, beyond them, He with Whom is the knowledge of all things in the preserved Tablet.

187   Whensoever the clouds of tribulation have rained down the darts of affliction in the path of God, the Lord of all names, I have hastened to meet them, as every fair-minded and discerning soul shall attest. How many the nights which found the beasts of the field resting in their lairs, and the birds of the air lying in their nests, while this Youth languished in chains and fetters with none to aid or succor Him!

188   Call Thou to mind God's mercy unto Thee; how, when Thou wert imprisoned with a number of other souls, He delivered Thee and aided Thee with the hosts of the seen and the unseen, until the King sent Thee to 'Iráq after We had disclosed unto him that Thou wert not of the sowers of sedition. Those who follow their corrupt desires and lay aside the fear of God are indeed in grievous error. They that

spread disorder in the land, shed the blood of men, and wrongfully consume the substance of others—We, verily, are clear of them, and We beseech God not to associate Us with them, whether in this world or in the world to come, unless they should repent unto Him. He, verily, is of those who show mercy the most merciful.

Whoso turneth towards God must distinguish himself    189 from others by his every deed, and follow that which hath been enjoined upon him in the Book. Thus hath it been decreed in a lucid Tablet. Those, however, who cast behind their backs the commandments of God, and follow the prompting of their own desires, are, verily, in grievous error.

O King! I adjure thee by thy Lord, the All-Merciful, to    190 look upon thy servants with the glances of the eye of thy favor, and to treat them with justice, that God may treat thee with mercy. Potent is thy Lord to do as He pleaseth. The world, with all its abasement and glory, shall pass away, and the kingdom will remain unto God, the Most Exalted, the All-Knowing.

Say: He hath kindled the lamp of utterance, and feedeth    191 it with the oil of wisdom and understanding. Too high is thy Lord, the All-Merciful, for aught in the universe to resist His Faith. He revealeth what He pleaseth through the power of His sovereign might, and protecteth it with a host of His well-favored angels. He is supreme over His servants and exerciseth undisputed dominion over His creation. He, verily, is the All-Knowing, the All-Wise.

O King! I was but a man like others, asleep upon My    192 couch, when lo, the breezes of the All-Glorious were wafted over Me, and taught Me the knowledge of all that hath been. This thing is not from Me, but from One Who is

Almighty and All-Knowing. And He bade Me lift up My voice between earth and heaven, and for this there befell Me what hath caused the tears of every man of understanding to flow. The learning current amongst men I studied not; their schools I entered not. Ask of the city wherein I dwelt, that thou mayest be well assured that I am not of them who speak falsely. This is but a leaf which the winds of the will of thy Lord, the Almighty, the All-Praised, have stirred. Can it be still when the tempestuous winds are blowing? Nay, by Him Who is the Lord of all Names and Attributes! They move it as they list. The evanescent is as nothing before Him Who is the Ever-Abiding. His all-compelling summons hath reached Me, and caused Me to speak His praise amidst all people. I was indeed as one dead when His behest was uttered. The hand of the will of thy Lord, the Compassionate, the Merciful, transformed Me. Can anyone speak forth of his own accord that for which all men, both high and low, will protest against him? Nay, by Him Who taught the Pen the eternal mysteries, save him whom the grace of the Almighty, the All-Powerful, hath strengthened.

193  The Pen of the Most High addresseth Me, saying: Fear not. Relate unto His Majesty the Sháh that which befell thee. His heart, verily, is between the fingers of thy Lord, the God of Mercy, that haply the sun of justice and bounty may shine forth above the horizon of his heart. Thus hath the decree been sent down by Him Who is the All-Wise.

194  Look upon this Youth, O King, with the eyes of justice; judge thou, then, with truth concerning what hath befallen Him. Of a verity, God hath made thee His shadow amongst men, and the sign of His power unto all that dwell on earth. Judge thou between Us and them that have wronged Us

without proof and without an enlightening Book. They that surround thee love thee for their own sakes, whereas this Youth loveth thee for thine own sake, and hath had no desire except to draw thee nigh unto the seat of grace, and to turn thee toward the right hand of justice. Thy Lord beareth witness unto that which I declare.

O King! Wert thou to incline thine ear unto the shrill   195
of the Pen of Glory and the cooing of the Dove of Eternity which, on the branches of the Lote-Tree beyond which there is no passing, uttereth praises to God, the Maker of all names and Creator of earth and heaven, thou wouldst attain unto a station from which thou wouldst behold in the world of being naught save the effulgence of the Adored One, and wouldst regard thy sovereignty as the most contemptible of thy possessions, abandoning it to whosoever might desire it, and setting thy face toward the Horizon aglow with the light of His countenance. Neither wouldst thou ever be willing to bear the burden of dominion save for the purpose of helping thy Lord, the Exalted, the Most High. Then would the Concourse on high bless thee. O how excellent is this most sublime station, couldst thou ascend thereunto through the power of a sovereignty recognized as derived from the Name of God!

Amongst the people are those who allege that this Youth   196
hath had no purpose but to perpetuate His name, whilst others claim that He hath sought for Himself the vanities of the world—this, notwithstanding that never, throughout all My days, have I found a place of safety, be it to the extent of a single foothold. At all times have I been immersed in an ocean of tribulations, whose full measure none can fathom but God. He, truly, is aware of what I say. How many the

days in which My loved ones have been sorely shaken by reason of My afflictions, and how many the nights during which My kindred, fearing for My life, have bitterly wept and lamented! And this none can deny save them that are bereft of truthfulness. Is it conceivable that He Who expecteth to lose His life at any moment should seek after worldly vanities? How very strange the imaginings of those who speak as prompted by their own caprices, and who wander distractedly in the wilderness of self and passion! Erelong shall they be called upon to account for their words, and on that day they shall find none to befriend or help them.

197 And amongst the people are those who claim that He hath disbelieved in God—yet every member of My body testifieth that there is none other God but Him; that those Whom He hath raised up in truth and sent forth with His guidance are the Manifestations of His most excellent names, the Revealers of His most exalted attributes, and the Repositories of His Revelation in the kingdom of creation; that through them the Proof of God hath been perfected unto all else but Him, the standard of Divine Unity hath been raised, and the sign of sanctity hath been made manifest; and that through them every soul hath found a path unto the Lord of the Throne on high. We testify that there is none other God but Him, that from everlasting He was alone with none else besides Him, and that He shall be unto everlasting what He hath ever been. Too high is the All-Merciful for the hearts of those who have recognized Him to apprehend His true nature, or for the minds of men to hope to fathom His essence. He verily is exalted above the understanding of anyone besides Himself, and sanctified beyond the compre-

hension of all else save Him. From all eternity He hath been independent of the entire creation.

Remember the days in which the Sun of Baṭḥá* shone     198 forth above the horizon of the Will of thy Lord, the Exalted, the Most High, and recall how the divines of that age turned away from Him, and the learned contended with Him, that haply thou mayest apprehend that which, in this day, remaineth concealed behind the veils of glory. So grievous became His plight on every side that He instructed His companions to disperse. Thus was the decree sent down from the heaven of divine glory. Remember, furthermore, how, when one of these same companions came before the King of Ethiopia and recited unto him a Súrih of the Qur'án, he declared to his attendants: "This, truly, hath been revealed by One Who is All-Knowing and All-Wise. Whoso acknowledgeth the truth, and believeth in the teachings of Jesus, can in no wise deny what hath been recited. We, verily, bear witness to its truth, even as we bear witness to the truth of that which we possess of the Books of God, the Help in Peril, the Self-Subsisting."

I swear by God, O King! Wert thou to incline thine ear     199 to the melodies of that Nightingale which warbleth in manifold accents upon the mystic bough as bidden by thy Lord, the All-Merciful, thou wouldst cast away thy sovereignty and set thy face towards this Scene of transcendent glory, this station above whose horizon shineth the Book of the Dawntide,[16] and wouldst expend all that thou possessest in thine eagerness to obtain the things of God. Then wouldst

---

* Muḥammad.

thou find thyself raised up to the summit of exaltation and glory, and elevated to the pinnacle of majesty and independence. Thus hath the decree been recorded in the Mother Book by the Pen of the All-Merciful. Of what avail are the things which are yours today and which tomorrow others shall possess? Choose for thyself that which God hath chosen for His elect, and God shall grant thee a mighty sovereignty in His Kingdom. We beseech God to aid thy Majesty to hearken unto that Word whose radiance hath enveloped the whole world, and to protect thee from such as have strayed far from the court of His presence.

200    Glory be to Thee, O Lord My God! How many the heads which were raised aloft on spears in Thy path, and how many the breasts which were made the target of arrows for the sake of Thy good pleasure! How many the hearts that have been lacerated for the exaltation of Thy Word and the promotion of Thy Cause, and how many the eyes that have wept sore for love of Thee! I implore Thee, O Thou Who art the King of kings and the Pitier of the downtrodden, by Thy Most Great Name which Thou hast made the Dawning-Place of Thy most excellent names and the Dayspring of Thy most exalted attributes, to remove the veils that have come in between Thee and Thy creatures and debarred them from turning unto the horizon of Thy Revelation. Cause them, then, O My God, by Thy most exalted Word, to turn from the left hand of oblivion and delusion unto the right hand of knowledge and certitude, that they may know what Thou hast purposed for them through Thy bounty and grace, and may set their faces towards Him Who is the Manifestation of Thy Cause and the Revealer of Thy signs.

O My God! Thou art the All-Bountiful, Whose grace is 201
infinite. Withhold not Thy servants from the most mighty
Ocean, which Thou hast made the repository of the pearls of
Thy knowledge and Thy wisdom, and turn them not away
from Thy gate, which Thou hast opened wide before all who
are in Thy heaven and all who are on Thy earth. O Lord!
Leave them not to themselves, for they understand not and
flee from that which is better for them than all that Thou
hast created upon Thine earth. Cast upon them, O My God,
the glances of the eye of Thy favor and bounty, and deliver
them from self and passion, that they may draw nigh unto
Thy most exalted Horizon, taste the sweetness of Thy remembrance, and delight in that bread which Thou hast sent
down from the heaven of Thy Will and the firmament of Thy
grace. From everlasting Thy bounty hath embraced the entire
creation and Thy mercy hath surpassed all things. No God is
there but Thee, the Ever-Forgiving, the Most Compassionate.

Glorified art Thou, O Lord My God! Thou well knowest 202
that Mine heart hath melted in Thy Cause, and that My
blood so boileth in My veins with the fire of Thy love that
every drop of it proclaimeth with its inner tongue: "Grant
that I may be spilt upon the ground for Thy sake, O my
Lord, the Most High, that from it there may spring forth
that which Thou hast purposed in Thy Tablets and hast hidden from the eyes of all, except such servants as have tasted
of the crystal stream of knowledge from the hands of Thy
grace and quaffed the soft-flowing waters of understanding
from the cup of Thy bestowal."

Thou knowest, O My God, that in all Mine affairs I have 203
sought only to obey Thy bidding, that in Mine every ut-

terance I have wished only to extol Thy praise, and that in whatsoever hath proceeded from My Pen I have purposed only to win Thy good pleasure and to reveal that which Thou hast enjoined upon Me through Thy sovereignty.

204    Thou beholdest Me, O My God, as one bewildered in Thy land. Whensoever I make mention of that which Thou hast enjoined upon Me, Thy creatures cavil at Me; yet were I to neglect that which Thou hast bidden Me observe, I would deserve the scourge of Thine anger and would be far removed from the meadows of Thy nearness. Nay, by Thy glory! I have set My face towards Thy good pleasure, and turned away from the things whereon Thy servants have set their affections. I have embraced all that is with Thee, and forsaken all that might lead Me away from the retreats of Thy nearness and the heights of Thy glory. I swear by Thy might! With Thy love in My heart nothing can ever alarm Me, and in the path of Thy good pleasure all the world's afflictions can in no wise dismay Me. All this, however, proceedeth from Thy power and Thy might, from Thy bounty and Thy grace, and is not of Mine own deserving.

205    This is an Epistle, O My God, which I have purposed to send unto the King. Thou knowest that I have wished of him naught but that he should show forth justice to Thy servants and extend his favors unto the people of Thy kingdom. For Myself I have desired only what Thou didst desire, and through Thy succor I wish for naught save that which Thou wishest. Perish the soul that seeketh from Thee aught save Thyself! I swear by Thy glory! Thy good pleasure is my dearest wish, and Thy purpose My highest hope. Have mercy, O My God, upon this poor creature Who hath clung unto the hem of Thy riches, and this suppliant soul Who

calleth upon Thee, saying, "Thou art, verily, the Lord of might and glory!" Assist Thou, O My God, His Majesty the Sháh to keep Thy statutes amidst Thy servants and to manifest Thy justice amongst Thy creatures, that he may treat this people as he treateth others. Thou art, in truth, the God of power, of glory and wisdom.

By the leave and permission of the King of the Age, this ²⁰⁶ Servant journeyed from the Seat of Sovereignty* to 'Iráq, and dwelt for twelve years in that land. Throughout the entire course of this period no account of Our condition was submitted to the court of thy presence, and no representation ever made to foreign powers. Placing Our whole trust in God, We resided in that land until there came to 'Iráq a certain official[17] who, upon his arrival, undertook to harass this poor company of exiles. Day after day, at the instigation of some of the outwardly learned and of other individuals, he would stir up trouble for these servants, although they had at no time committed any act detrimental to the state and its people or contrary to the rules and customs of the citizens of the realm.

Fearing lest the actions of these transgressors should ²⁰⁷ produce some outcome at variance with thy world-adorning judgment, this Servant dispatched a brief account of the matter to Mírzá Sa'íd Khán[18] at the Foreign Ministry, so that he might submit it to the royal presence and that whatever thou shouldst please to decree in this respect might be obeyed. A long while elapsed, and no decree was issued. Finally matters came to such a pass that there loomed the

---

* Ṭihrán.

threat of imminent strife and bloodshed. Of necessity, therefore, and for the protection of the servants of God, a few of them appealed to the Governor of 'Iráq.[19]

208   Wert thou to observe these events with the eye of fairness, it would become clear and evident in the luminous mirror of thine heart that what occurred was called for by the circumstances, and that no other alternative could be seen. His Majesty himself is witness that in whatever city a number of this people have resided, the hostility of certain functionaries hath enkindled the flame of conflict and contention. This evanescent Soul, however, hath, since His arrival in 'Iráq, forbidden all to engage in dissension and strife. The witness of this Servant is His very deeds, for all are well aware and will testify that, although a greater number of this people resided in 'Iráq than in any other land, no one overstepped his limits or transgressed against his neighbor. Fixing their gaze upon God, and reposing their trust in Him, all have now been abiding in peace for well-nigh fifteen years, and, in whatever hath befallen them, they have shown forth patience and resigned themselves to God.

209   After the arrival of this Servant in this, the city of Adrianople, some of the people of 'Iráq and elsewhere inquired about the meaning of the term "rendering assistance unto God" which hath been mentioned in the Holy Scriptures. Several answers were sent out in reply, one of which is set forth in these pages, that it may be clearly demonstrated in the court of thy presence that this Servant hath had no end in view but to promote the betterment and well-being of the world. And if certain of the divine favors which, undeserving as I may be, God hath pleased to bestow upon Me be not plain and manifest, this much at least will be clear and ap-

parent, that He, in His surpassing mercy and infinite grace, hath not deprived Mine heart of the ornament of reason. The passage that was referred to concerning the meaning of "rendering assistance unto God" is as follows:

*He is God, exalted be His glory!*

It is clear and evident that the one true God—glorified be His mention!—is sanctified above the world and all that is therein. By "rendering assistance unto God," then, it is not meant that any soul should fight or contend with another. That Sovereign Lord Who doeth whatsoever He pleaseth hath entrusted the kingdom of creation, its lands and its seas, into the hands of the kings, for they are, each according to his degree, the manifestations of His divine power. Should they enter beneath the shadow of the True One, they will be accounted of God, and if not, thy Lord, verily, knoweth and observeth all things. 210

That which God—glorified be His Name!—hath desired for Himself is the hearts of His servants, which are the treasuries of His love and remembrance and the repositories of His knowledge and wisdom. It hath ever been the wish of the Eternal King to cleanse the hearts of His servants from the things of the world and all that pertaineth thereunto, that they may be made worthy recipients of the effulgent splendors of Him Who is the King of all names and attributes. Wherefore must no stranger be allowed in the city of the heart, that the incomparable Friend may enter His abode. By this is meant the effulgence of His names and attributes, and not His exalted Essence, inasmuch 211 as that peerless King hath ever been, and shall eternally remain, sanctified above ascent and descent.

212   It followeth, therefore, that rendering assistance unto God, in this day, doth not and shall never consist in contending or disputing with any soul; nay rather, what is preferable in the sight of God is that the cities of men's hearts, which are ruled by the hosts of self and passion, should be subdued by the sword of utterance, of wisdom and of understanding. Thus, whoso seeketh to assist God must, before all else, conquer, with the sword of inner meaning and explanation, the city of his own heart and guard it from the remembrance of all save God, and only then set out to subdue the cities of the hearts of others.

213   Such is the true meaning of rendering assistance unto God. Sedition hath never been pleasing unto God, nor were the acts committed in the past by certain foolish ones acceptable in His sight. Know ye that to be killed in the path of His good pleasure is better for you than to kill. The beloved of the Lord must, in this day, behave in such wise amidst His servants that they may by their very deeds and actions guide all men unto the paradise of the All-Glorious.

214   By Him Who shineth above the Dayspring of Sanctity! The friends of God have not, nor will they ever, set their hopes upon the world and its ephemeral possessions. The one true God hath ever regarded the hearts of men as His own, His exclusive possession—and this too but as an expression of His all-surpassing mercy, that haply mortal souls may be purged and sanctified from all that pertaineth to the world of dust and gain

admittance into the realms of eternity. For otherwise that ideal King is, in Himself and by Himself, sufficient unto Himself and independent of all things. Neither doth the love of His creatures profit Him, nor can their malice harm Him. All have issued forth from abodes of dust, and unto dust shall they return, while the one true God, alone and single, is established upon His Throne, a Throne which is beyond the reaches of time and space, is sanctified above all utterance or expression, intimation, description and definition, and is exalted beyond all notion of abasement and glory. And none knoweth this save Him and those with whom is the knowledge of the Book. No God is there but Him, the Almighty, the All-Bountiful.

It behooveth the benevolence of the Sovereign, however, to examine all matters with the eye of justice and mercy, and not to content himself with the baseless claims of certain individuals. We beseech God to graciously assist the King to fulfil that which He pleaseth, and, verily, that which He desireth should be the desire of all the worlds. 215

Later this Servant was summoned to Constantinople, whither We arrived accompanied by a poor band of exiles. At no time thereafter did We seek to meet with anyone, as We had no request to make and no aim in view but to demonstrate unto all that this Servant had no mischief in mind and had never associated with the sowers of sedition. By Him Who hath caused the tongues of all beings to speak forth His praise! While certain considerations rendered it difficult to make application to any quarter, such steps were perforce taken to protect certain souls. My Lord, verily, 216 knoweth what is in Me, and He beareth witness unto the truth of what I say.

217  A just king is the shadow of God on earth. All should seek shelter under the shadow of his justice, and rest in the shade of his favor. This is not a matter which is either specific or limited in its scope, that it might be restricted to one or another person, inasmuch as the shadow telleth of the One Who casteth it. God, glorified be His remembrance, hath called Himself the Lord of the worlds, for He hath nurtured and still nurtureth everyone. Glorified be, then, His grace that hath preceded all created things, and His mercy that hath surpassed the worlds.

218  It is clear and evident that, whether this Cause be seen as right or wrong by the people, those who are associated with its name have accepted and embraced it as true, and have forsaken their all in their eagerness to partake of the things of God. That they should evince such renunciation in the path of the love of the All-Merciful is in itself a faithful witness and an eloquent testimony to the truth of their convictions. Hath it ever been witnessed that a man of sound judgment should sacrifice his life without cause or reason? And if it be suggested that this people have taken leave of their senses, this too is highly improbable, inasmuch as such behavior hath not been confined to merely a soul or two—nay, a vast multitude of every class have drunk their fill of the living waters of divine knowledge, and, intoxicated, have hastened with heart and soul to the field of sacrifice in the way of the Beloved.

219  If these souls, who have renounced all else but God for His sake and offered up their life and substance in His path, are to be accounted as false, then by what proof and tes-

timony can the truth of what others assert be established in thy presence? The late Ḥájí Siyyid Muḥammad[20]—may God exalt his station and immerse him in the ocean of His forgiveness and mercy!—was one of the most learned divines of his age, and one of the most devout and pious men of his time. So highly was he regarded that his praise was on every tongue, and his righteousness and piety were universally acknowledged. Yet, when hostilities broke out with Russia,[21] he who himself had pronounced the decree of holy war, and who with blazoned standard had left his native land to rally to the support of his faith, abandoned, after the inconvenience of a brief encounter, all the good that he had purposed, and returned whence he had come. Would that the veil might be lifted, and that which hath ere now remained hidden from the eyes of men be made manifest!

For more than twenty years this people have, day and night, been subjected to the fury of the Sovereign's wrath, and have been scattered by the tempestuous gales of his displeasure, each to a different land. How many the children who have been left fatherless, and how many the fathers who have lost their sons! How many the mothers who have dared not, out of fear and dread, to mourn their slaughtered offspring! How numerous those who, at eventide, were possessed of utmost wealth and affluence, and who, when morning came, had fallen into utter abasement and destitution! No land is there whose soil hath not been tinged with their blood, nor reach of heaven unto which their sighs have not ascended. Throughout the years the darts of affliction have unceasingly rained down from the clouds of God's decree, yet despite all these calamities and tribulations, the flame of divine love hath so blazed in their hearts that even

220

97

should their bodies be torn asunder they would not forsake their love of Him Who is the Best-Beloved of the worlds, but would welcome with heart and soul whatever might befall them in the path of God.

221     O King! The breezes of the grace of the All-Merciful have transformed these servants and attracted them unto His Holy Court. "The witness of a true lover is upon his sleeve." Nevertheless, some of the outwardly learned have troubled the luminous heart of the King of the Age concerning these souls who revolve round the Tabernacle of the All-Merciful and who seek to attain the Sanctuary of true knowledge. Would that the world-adorning wish of His Majesty might decree that this Servant be brought face to face with the divines of the age, and produce proofs and testimonies in the presence of His Majesty the Sháh! This Servant is ready, and taketh hope in God, that such a gathering may be convened in order that the truth of the matter may be made clear and manifest before His Majesty the Sháh. It is then for thee to command, and I stand ready before the throne of thy sovereignty. Decide, then, for Me or against Me.

222     The All-Merciful saith in the Qur'án, His abiding testimony unto all the peoples of the world: "Wish ye then for death, if ye be men of truth."[22] Behold how He hath declared the yearning for death to be the touchstone of sincerity! And, in the luminous mirror of thy judgment, it is doubtless clear and evident which people have chosen, in this day, to lay down their lives in the path of the Beloved of the worlds. Indeed, were the books supporting the beliefs of this people to be written with the blood spilled in the path of God—exalted be His glory!—then countless volumes would have already appeared amongst men for all to see.

How, We fain would ask, is it possible to impugn this    223
people whose deeds are in conformity with their words, and
to give credence instead to those who have refused to relin-
quish one jot of their worldly authority in the path of Him
Who is the Unconstrained? Some of the divines who have
declared this Servant an infidel have at no time met with
Me. Never having seen Me, or become acquainted with My
purpose, they have nevertheless spoken as they pleased and
acted as they desired. Yet every claim requireth a proof, not
mere words and displays of outward piety.

In this connection the text of several passages from the    224
Hidden Book of Fáṭimih—the blessings of God be upon
her!—which are relevant to the present theme will be cited in the Persian tongue, that certain matters which have
ere now been hidden may be revealed before thy presence.
The people addressed in the aforementioned Book, which is
today known as the Hidden Words, are those who, though
outwardly known for learning and piety, are inwardly the
slaves of self and passion.

He saith: O ye that are foolish, yet have a name to be    225
wise! Wherefore do ye wear the guise of the shepherd, when
inwardly ye have become wolves, intent upon My flock? Ye
are even as the star, which riseth ere the dawn, and which,
though it seem radiant and luminous, leadeth the wayfarers
of My city astray into the paths of perdition.

And likewise He saith: O ye seeming fair yet inwardly foul!    226
Ye are like clear but bitter water, which to outward seeming is
crystal pure but of which, when tested by the Divine Assayer,
not a drop is accepted. Yea, the sunbeam falls alike upon the
dust and the mirror, yet differ they in reflection even as doth
the star from the earth: nay, immeasurable is the difference!

227 And also He saith: O essence of desire! At many a dawn have I turned from the realms of the Placeless unto thine abode, and found thee on the bed of ease busied with others than Myself. Thereupon, even as the flash of the spirit, I returned to the realms of celestial glory, and breathed it not in My retreats above unto the hosts of holiness.

228 And again He saith: O bondslave of the world! Many a dawn hath the breeze of My loving-kindness wafted over thee and found thee upon the bed of heedlessness fast asleep. Bewailing then thy plight it returned whence it came.[23]

229 Therefore, in the exercise of the royal justice, it is not sufficient to give ear to the claimant alone. God saith in the Qur'án, the unerring Balance that distinguisheth truth from falsehood: "O ye who believe! If a wicked man come to you with news, clear it up at once, lest through ignorance ye harm others, and afterward repent of what ye have done."[24] The holy Traditions, moreover, contain the admonition: "Believe not the tale-bearer." Certain of the divines, who have never seen Us, have misconceived the nature of Our Cause. Those, however, who have met Us will testify that this Servant hath not spoken save in accordance with that which God hath commanded in the Book, and that He hath called attention to the following blessed verse—exalted be His Word: "Do ye not disavow us only because we believe in God, and in what He hath sent down unto us, and in what He had sent down aforetime?"[25]

230 O King of the age! The eyes of these refugees are turned towards and fixed upon the mercy of the Most Merciful. No doubt is there whatever that these tribulations will be followed by the outpourings of a supreme mercy, and these dire adversities will be succeeded by an overflowing pros-

perity. We fain would hope, however, that His Majesty the Sháh will himself examine these matters and bring hope to the hearts. That which We have submitted to thy Majesty is indeed for thine highest good. And God, verily, is a sufficient witness unto Me.

Glorified art Thou, O Lord My God! I bear witness that    231
the heart of the King is in truth between the fingers of Thy might. If it be Thy wish, do Thou incline it, O My God, in the direction of charity and mercy. Thou, verily, art the Almighty, the Most Exalted, the Most Bountiful. No God is there besides Thee, the All-Glorious, the One Whose help is sought by all.

Concerning the prerequisites of the learned, He saith:    232
"Whoso among the learned guardeth his self, defendeth his faith, opposeth his desires, and obeyeth his Lord's command, it is incumbent upon the generality of the people to pattern themselves after him. . . ."[26] Should the King of the Age reflect upon this utterance which hath streamed from the tongue of Him Who is the Dayspring of the Revelation of the All-Merciful, he would perceive that those who have been adorned with the attributes enumerated in this holy Tradition are scarcer than the philosopher's stone; wherefore not every man that layeth claim to knowledge deserveth to be believed.

Again concerning the divines of the Latter Days, He saith:    233
"The religious doctors of that age shall be the most wicked of the divines beneath the shadow of heaven. Out of them hath mischief proceeded, and unto them it shall return." And again He saith: "When the Standard of Truth is made manifest, the people of both the East and the West curse it."[27] Should anyone dispute these Traditions, this Servant

will undertake to establish their validity, since the details of their transmission have been omitted here for the sake of brevity.

234     Those doctors who have indeed drunk of the cup of renunciation have never interfered with this Servant. Thus, for example, Shaykh Murtadá[28]—may God exalt his station and cause him to repose beneath the canopy of His grace!—showed forth kindness during Our sojourn in 'Iráq, and never spoke of this Cause otherwise than as God hath given leave. We beseech God to graciously assist all to do His will and pleasure.

235     Now, however, all have lost sight of every other consideration, and are bent upon the persecution of this people. Thus, if it be inquired of certain persons who, by the grace of their Lord, repose beneath the shadow of thy royal mercy and enjoy countless favors, "What service have ye rendered in return for these royal favors? Have ye through wise policy annexed a further territory to the realm? Have ye applied yourselves to aught that would secure the welfare of the people, the prosperity of the kingdom, and the lasting glory of the state?," they will have no other reply than to designate, justly or falsely, a group of people before thy royal presence as Bábís, and forthwith to engage in massacre and pillage. In Tabríz, for instance, and in the Egyptian town of Manṣúríyyih, a number of this people were ransomed and large sums were seized, yet no account of these matters was ever made in the court of thy presence.

236     The reason for which all these things have come to pass is that their persecutors, finding these unfortunate ones without protection, have forgone more weighty matters and occupied themselves instead with harassing this afflict-

ed people. Numerous confessions and divers creeds abide peacefully beneath the shadow of thy sovereignty. Let this people be also numbered with them. Nay, those who serve the King should be animated by such lofty aims and sublime intentions as to continually strive to bring all religions beneath the shelter of his shadow, and to rule over them with perfect justice.

To enforce the laws of God is naught but justice, and is the source of universal content. Nay more, the divine statutes have always been, and will ever remain, the cause and instrument of the preservation of mankind, as witnessed by His exalted words: "In punishment will ye find life, O men of insight!"[29] It would, however, ill beseem the justice of thy Majesty that for the trespass of a single soul a whole group of people should be subjected to the scourge of thy wrath. The one true God—glorified be His Name!—hath said: "None shall bear the burden of another."[30] It is clear and evident that in every community there have been, and will ever be, the learned and the ignorant, the wise and the heedless, the profligate and the pious. That a wise and reflecting soul should commit a heinous deed is most improbable, inasmuch as such a person either seeketh after this world or hath forsaken it: If he be of the latter, he would assuredly have no regard for aught else besides God, and moreover the fear of God would deter him from unlawful and reprehensible actions; and if he be of the former, he would just as assuredly avoid such deeds as would alienate and alarm the people, and act in such a manner as to earn their confidence and trust. It is therefore evident that reprehensible actions have always emanated, and will ever emanate, from ignorant and foolish souls. We implore God to guard His servants from

237

turning to anyone save Him, and to draw them nigh unto His presence. His might, in truth, is equal to all things.

238     Praise be unto Thee, O Lord My God! Thou hearest the voice of My lamentation, and beholdest My condition, My distress and affliction! Thou knowest all that is in Me. If the call I have raised be wholly for Thy sake, then draw thereby the hearts of Thy creatures towards the heaven of Thy knowledge, and the heart of the Sovereign towards the right hand of the throne of Thy name, the All-Merciful. Supply him then, O My God, with a portion of that goodly sustenance which hath descended from the heaven of Thy generosity and the clouds of Thy mercy, that he may forsake his all and turn unto the court of Thy favor. Aid him, O My God, to assist Thy Cause and to exalt Thy Word amidst Thy creatures. Strengthen him, then, with the hosts of the seen and the unseen, that he may subdue every city in Thy Name, and hold sway, through Thy sovereignty and might, over all that dwell on earth, O Thou in Whose hand is the kingdom of creation! Thou, verily, art the Supreme Ordainer in both the beginning and the end. No God is there but Thee, the Most Powerful, the All-Glorious, the All-Wise.

239     So grossly hath Our Cause been misrepresented before thy royal presence that, if some unseemly act be committed by but one of this people, it is portrayed as being prompted by their beliefs. By Him besides Whom there is none other God! This Servant hath refused even to sanction the commission of reproved actions, how much less those which have been explicitly prohibited in the Book of God.

240     God hath forbidden unto men the drinking of wine, and this prohibition hath been revealed and recorded in His Book. In spite of this, and of the fact that the learned doc-

tors of the age—may God increase their numbers!—have all prohibited the people from such a wretched act, there still remain some who commit it. The punishment which this act entaileth, however, applieth only to its heedless perpetrators, whilst those noble manifestations of supreme sanctity remain exalted above and exempt from all blame. Yea, the whole creation, both seen and unseen, beareth witness unto their holiness.

Yea, these servants regard the one true God as He Who "doeth as He willeth"[31] and "ordaineth as He pleaseth."[32] Thus they view not as impossible the continued appearance in the contingent world of the Manifestations of His Unity. Should anyone hold otherwise, how would he be different from those who believe the hand of God to be "chained up"?[33] And if the one true God—glorified be His mention!—be indeed regarded as unconstrained, then whatever Cause that Ancient King may please to manifest from the wellspring of His Command must be embraced by all. No refuge is there for anyone and no haven to hasten unto save God; no protection is there for any soul and no shelter to seek except in Him.

The essential requirement for whoso advanceth a claim is to support his assertions with clear proofs and testimonies. Beyond this, the rejection of the people, whether learned or ignorant, hath never been, nor shall it ever be, of any consequence. The Prophets of God, those Pearls of the ocean of Divine Unity and the Repositories of Divine Revelation, have ever been the object of men's repudiation and denial. Even as He saith: "Each nation hath plotted darkly against their Messenger to lay violent hold on Him, and disputed with vain words to invalidate the truth."[34] And again:

"No Messenger cometh unto them but they laugh Him to scorn."[35]

243     Consider the dispensation of Him Who is the Seal of the Prophets and the King of the Chosen Ones—may the souls of all mankind be offered up for His sake! After the Daystar of Truth dawned above the horizon of Ḥijáz, how great were the cruelties which the exponents of error inflicted upon that incomparable Manifestation of the All-Glorious! Such was their heedlessness that they regarded every injury inflicted upon that sacred Being as ranking among the greatest of all acts, and constituting a means of attainment unto God, the Most High. For in the early years of His mission the divines of that age, both Christian and Jewish, turned away from that Daystar of the heaven of glory, whereupon all people, high and low alike, bestirred themselves to extinguish the light of that Luminary of the horizon of inner meanings. The names of all these divines have been mentioned in the books of old; among them are Wahb ibn-i-Ráhib, Kaʻb ibn-i-Ashraf, ʻAbdu'lláh-i-Ubayy, and others of their like.

244     Finally, matters came to such a pass that these men took counsel together and conspired to shed His pure blood, even as God—glorified be His mention!—saith: "And remember when the disbelievers schemed against Thee, that they might lay hold upon Thee, or slay Thee, or cast Thee out; and so they schemed, and God schemed, and God, verily, is the best of schemers."[36] Again He saith: "But if their opposition be grievous to Thee—if Thou canst, seek out an opening into the earth or a ladder into heaven and bring to them a sign; yet if God wished, He could gather them unto true guidance; be Thou not, then, of the ignorant."[37] By God! The hearts of His favored ones are consumed at the purport

of these two blessed verses. Such established and undisputed facts have been forgotten, and no one hath paused to reflect, in days past or in this day, upon the things that have prompted men to turn away from the Revealers of the light of God at the time of their manifestation.

Likewise, before the appearance of the Seal of the Prophets, consider Jesus, the Son of Mary. When that Manifestation of the All-Merciful revealed Himself, all the divines charged that Quintessence of faith with impiety and rebellion. Eventually, with the sanction of Annas, the most learned of the divines of His day, and Caiaphas, the high priest, His blessed person was made to suffer that which the pen is ashamed to mention and powerless to describe. The wide world in all its vastness could no longer contain Him, until at last God raised Him up unto heaven. 245

Were a detailed account of all the Prophets to be given here, We fear that it might lead to weariness. The doctors of the Torah in particular assert that no independent Prophet will come after Moses with a new Law. They maintain that a Scion of the House of David shall be made manifest Who will promulgate the Law of the Torah, and help establish and enforce its commandments throughout the East and the West. 246

The followers of the Gospel, likewise, hold as impossible that the Bearer of a new Revelation should again shine forth from the dayspring of the Will of God after Jesus, Son of Mary—peace be upon Him! In support of this contention, they adduce the following verse from the Gospel: "Heaven and earth shall pass away, but the words of the Son of Man shall never pass away."[38] They maintain that neither the teachings nor the commandments of Jesus—peace be upon Him!—may ever be altered. 247

248     At one point in the Gospel, He saith: "I go away, and come again."[39] Again in the Gospel of John, He hath foretold the advent of a Comforter who shall come after Him.[40] In the Gospel of Luke, moreover, a number of signs and portents have been mentioned. Certain divines of that Faith, however, have interpreted these utterances after their own fancy, and have thus failed to grasp their true significance.

249     O would that thou wouldst permit Me, O Sháh, to send unto thee that which would cheer the eyes, and tranquillize the souls, and persuade every fair-minded person that with Him is the knowledge of the Book. Certain persons, incapable of answering the objections raised by their opponents, claim that the Torah and the Gospel have been corrupted, whereas in reality the references to such corruption pertain only to specific cases.[41] But for the repudiation of the foolish and the connivance of the divines, I would have uttered a discourse that would have thrilled and carried away the hearts unto a realm from the murmur of whose winds can be heard: "No God is there but He!" For the present, however, since the season is not ripe, the tongue of My utterance hath been stilled and the wine of exposition sealed up until such time as God, through the power of His might, shall please to unseal it. He, verily, is the Almighty, the Most Powerful.

250     Praise be unto Thee, O Lord My God! I ask Thee by Thy Name, through which Thou hast subdued all who are in the heavens and all who are on the earth, to protect the lamp of Thy Cause within the globe of Thine omnipotence and Thy bountiful favor, lest it be exposed to the blasts of denial from those who remain heedless of the mysteries of Thy name, the Unconstrained. Increase, then, by the oil of Thy wisdom, the radiance of its light. Thou, verily, hast power over all the dwellers of Thine earth and of Thy heaven.

I implore Thee, O My Lord, by that most exalted Word   251
which hath struck terror into the hearts of all who are in the
heavens and on the earth, save only those who have taken
fast hold of Thy Sure Handle, not to abandon Me amidst
Thy creatures. Lift Me up, then, unto Thyself, cause Me
to enter beneath the shadow of Thy mercy, and give Me
to drink of the pure wine of Thy providence, that I may
dwell within the tabernacle of Thy majesty and beneath the
canopy of Thy favor. Potent art Thou to do what pleaseth
Thee. Thou, verily, art the Help in Peril, the Self-Subsisting.

O King! The lamps of equity have been extinguished,   252
and the fire of tyranny hath so blazed on every side that
My people have been led as captives from Zawrá'*to Mosul,
known as Ḥadbá'. This is not the first outrage that hath
been suffered in the path of God. It behooveth every soul to
consider and call to mind that which befell the kindred of
the Prophet when the people took them captive and brought
them unto Damascus, known as Fayḥá'. Amongst them was
the prince of them that worship God, the mainstay of such
as have drawn nigh unto Him, and the sanctuary of those
who long for His presence—may the life of all else be a
sacrifice unto him![42]

They were asked: "Are ye of the party of the Seceders?"[43] He   253
replied: "Nay, by the Lord Almighty. We are but servants who
have believed in God and in His verses. Through us the countenance of faith hath beamed with joy. Through us the sign
of the All-Merciful hath shone forth. At the mention of our
names the desert of Baṭḥá** hath overflowed with water and
the darkness separating earth and heaven hath been dispelled."

---

* Baghdád.
** Mecca.

254   "Have ye forbidden," they were asked, "that which God hath made lawful, or allowed that which He hath forbidden?" "We were the first to follow the divine commandments," he answered. "We are the root and origin of His Cause, the beginning of all good and its end. We are the sign of the Ancient of Days and the source of His remembrance amongst the nations."

255   They were asked: "Have ye forsaken the Qur'án?" "In our House," he replied, "did the All-Merciful reveal it. We are the breezes of the All-Glorious amidst His creation. We are the streams that have branched out from the Most Great Ocean, through which God hath revived the earth, and through which He shall revive it again after it hath died. Through us His signs have been diffused, His proofs revealed, and His tokens disclosed. With us is the knowledge of His hidden meanings and His untold mysteries."

256   "For what crime have ye been punished?" they were asked. "For our love of God," he made reply, "and for our detachment from aught else save Him."

257   We have not related his exact words—peace be upon him!—but rather have We imparted a sprinkling from that ocean of life eternal that lieth enshrined within them, that those who hearken thereunto may be quickened and made aware of what hath befallen the trusted ones of God at the hands of a lost and wayward generation. We see the people in this day censuring the oppressors of bygone ages, whilst they themselves commit yet greater wrongs and know it not!

258   God beareth Me witness that My purpose hath not been to foment sedition, but to purify His servants from whatsoever hath prevented them from drawing nigh unto Him, the Lord of the Day of Reckoning. I was asleep upon My couch,

when lo, the breezes of My Lord, the All-Merciful, passed over Me, awoke Me from My slumber, and bade Me lift up My voice betwixt earth and heaven. This thing is not from Me, but from God. Unto this testify the dwellers of His Dominion and of His Kingdom, and the inhabitants of the cities of His unfading glory. By Him Who is the Truth! I fear no tribulation in His path, nor any affliction in My love for Him and in the way of His good pleasure. Verily God hath made adversity as a morning dew upon His green pasture, and a wick for His lamp which lighteth earth and heaven.

Shall a man's wealth endure forever, or protect him from   259 the One Who shall, erelong, seize him by his forelock? Gazing upon those who sleep beneath the gravestones, embosomed in the dust, could one ever distinguish the sovereign's crumbling skull from the subject's moldering bones? Nay, by Him Who is the King of kings! Could one discern the lord from the vassal, or those that enjoyed wealth and riches from those who possessed neither shoes nor mat? By God! Every distinction hath been erased, save only for those who upheld the right and who ruled with justice.

Whither are gone the learned men, the divines and po-   260 tentates of old? What hath become of their discriminating views, their shrewd perceptions, their subtle insights and sage pronouncements? Where are their hidden coffers, their flaunted ornaments, their gilded couches, their rugs and cushions strewn about? Gone forever is their generation! All have perished, and, by God's decree, naught remaineth of them but scattered dust. Exhausted is the wealth they gathered, dispersed the stores they hoarded, dissipated the treasures they concealed. Naught can now be seen but their deserted haunts, their roofless dwellings, their uprooted tree-trunks, and their faded splendor. No man of insight will let wealth distract his gaze from his ultimate objective, and no man of understanding will allow riches to withhold him from turning unto Him Who is the All-Possessing, the Most High.

261     Where is he who held dominion over all whereon the sun shineth, who lived extravagantly on earth, seeking out the luxuries of the world and of all that hath been created upon it? Where is the commander of the swarthy legion and the upraiser of the golden standard? Where is the ruler of Zawrá', and where the tyrant of Fayḥá'?⁴⁴ Where are those before whose munificence the treasure-houses of the earth shrank in shame, and at whose largesse and swelling spirit the very ocean was abashed? Where is he who stretched forth his arm in rebellion, and who turned his hand against the All-Merciful?

262     Where are they who went in quest of earthly pleasures and the fruits of carnal desires? Whither are fled their fair and comely women? Where are their swaying branches, their spreading boughs, their lofty mansions, their trellised gardens? And what of the delights of these gardens—their exquisite grounds and gentle breezes, their purling streams, their soughing winds, their cooing doves and rustling leaves? Where now are their resplendent morns and their brightsome countenances wreathed in smiles? Alas for them! All have perished and are gone to rest beneath a canopy of dust. Of them one heareth neither name nor mention; none knoweth of their affairs, and naught remaineth of their signs.

263     What! Will the people dispute then that whereof they themselves stand witness? Will they deny that which they

know to be true? I know not in what wilderness they roam! Do they not see that they are embarked upon a journey from which there is no return? How long will they wander from mountain to valley, from hollow to hill? "Hath not the time come for those who believe to humble their hearts at the mention of God?"[45] Blessed is he who hath said, or now shall say, "Yea, by my Lord! The time is come and the hour hath struck!," and who, thereafter, shall detach himself from all that hath been, and deliver himself up entirely unto Him Who is the Possessor of the universe and the Lord of all creation.

And yet, what hope! For naught is reaped save that which hath been sown, and naught is taken up save that which hath been laid down,[46] unless it be through the grace and bestowal of the Lord. Hath the womb of the world yet conceived one whom the veils of glory shall not hinder from ascending unto the Kingdom of his Lord, the All-Glorious, the Most High? Is it yet within us to perform such deeds as will dispel our afflictions and draw us nigh unto Him Who is the Causer of causes? We beseech God to deal with us according to His bounty, and not His justice, and to grant that we may be of those who have turned their faces unto their Lord and severed themselves from all else. 264

I have seen, O Sháh, in the path of God what eye hath not seen nor ear heard. Mine acquaintances have repudiated Me, and My pathways have been straitened. The fount of well-being hath run dry, and the bower of ease hath withered. How numerous the tribulations which have rained, and will soon rain, upon Me! I advance with My face set towards Him Who is the Almighty, the All-Bounteous, whilst 265 behind Me glideth the serpent. Mine eyes have rained down tears until My bed is drenched.

266 I sorrow not for Myself, however. By God! Mine head yearneth for the spear out of love for its Lord. I never passed a tree, but Mine heart addressed it saying: "O would that thou wert cut down in My name, and My body crucified upon thee, in the path of My Lord!," for I see the people wandering distraught and unconscious in their drunken stupor. They have raised on high their passions and set down their God. Methinks they have taken His Cause for a mockery and regard it as a play and pastime, believing all the while that they do well, and that they dwell securely in the citadel of safety. Howbeit the matter is not as they fondly imagine: Tomorrow shall they behold that which today they are wont to deny!

267 Erelong shall the exponents of wealth and power banish Us from the land of Adrianople to the city of 'Akká. According to what they say, it is the most desolate of the cities of the world, the most unsightly of them in appearance, the most detestable in climate, and the foulest in water. It is as though it were the metropolis of the owl, within whose precincts naught can be heard save the echo of its cry. Therein have they resolved to imprison this Youth, to shut against our faces the doors of ease and comfort, and to deprive us of every worldly benefit throughout the remainder of our days.

268 By God! Though weariness lay Me low, and hunger consume Me, and the bare rock be My bed, and My fellows the beasts of the field, I will not complain, but will endure patiently as those endued with constancy and firmness have endured patiently, through the power of God, the Eternal King and Creator of the nations, and will render thanks

unto God under all conditions. We pray that, out of His bounty—exalted be He—He may release, through this imprisonment, the necks of men from chains and fetters, and cause them to turn, with sincere faces, towards His face, Who is the Mighty, the Bounteous. Ready is He to answer whosoever calleth upon Him, and nigh is He unto such as commune with Him. We further beseech Him to make of this darksome tribulation a shield for the Temple of His Cause, and to protect it from the assault of sharpened swords and pointed daggers. Adversity hath ever given rise to the exaltation of His Cause and the glorification of His Name. Such hath been God's method carried into effect in centuries and ages past. That which the people now fail to apprehend they shall erelong discover, on that day when their steeds shall stumble and their finery be folded up, their blades blunted and their feet made to falter.

I know not how long they shall spur on the charger of 269 self and passion and rove in the wilderness of error and negligence! Shall either the pomp of the mighty or the wretchedness of the abased endure? Shall he who reposeth upon the loftiest seat of honor, who hath attained the pinnacle of might and glory, abide forever? Nay, by My Lord, the All-Merciful! All on earth shall pass away, and there remaineth alone the face of My Lord, the All-Glorious, the Most Bountiful.[47]

What armor hath not been pierced by the arrow of destruction, and what regal brow not divested by the hand of 270 Fate? What fortress hath withstood the approach of the Messenger of Death? What throne hath not been shattered to pieces, what palace not reduced to rubble? Could the people but taste that choice Wine of the mercy of their Lord, the

Almighty, the All-Knowing, which lieth in store for them in the world beyond, they would assuredly cease their censure, and seek only to win the good pleasure of this Youth. For now, however, they have hidden Me behind a veil of darkness, whose fabric they have woven with the hands of idle fancy and vain imagination. Erelong shall the snow-white hand of God rend an opening through the darkness of this night and unlock a mighty portal unto His City. On that Day shall the people enter therein by troops, uttering what the blamers aforetime exclaimed,[48] that there shall be made manifest in the end that which appeared in the beginning.

271 Is it their wish to tarry here when already they have one foot in the stirrup? Look they to return, once they are gone? Nay, by Him Who is the Lord of Lords! save on the Day of Judgment, the Day whereon the people shall arise from their graves and be asked of their legacy. Well is it with him who shall not be weighted down with his burdens on that Day, the Day whereon the mountains shall pass away and all shall gather to be questioned in the presence of God, the Most Exalted. Stern, indeed, is He in punishing!

272 We beseech God to purge the hearts of certain divines from rancor and enmity, that they may look upon matters with an eye unbeclouded by contempt. May He raise them up unto so lofty a station that neither the attractions of the world, nor the allurements of authority, may deflect them from gazing upon the Supreme Horizon, and that neither worldly benefits nor carnal desires shall prevent them from attaining that Day whereon the mountains shall be reduced to dust. Though they now rejoice in the adversity that hath befallen Us, soon shall come a day whereon they shall lament and weep. By My Lord! Were I given the choice between,

on the one hand, the wealth and opulence, the ease and comfort, the honor and glory which they enjoy, and, on the other, the adversities and trials which are Mine, I would unhesitatingly choose My present condition and would refuse to barter a single atom of these hardships for all that hath been created in the world of being.

But for the tribulations that have touched Me in the path 273 of God, life would have held no sweetness for Me, and Mine existence would have profited Me nothing. For them who are endued with discernment, and whose eyes are fixed upon the Sublime Vision, it is no secret that I have been, most of the days of My life, even as a slave, sitting under a sword hanging on a thread, knowing not whether it would fall soon or late upon him. And yet, notwithstanding all this We render thanks unto God, the Lord of the worlds, and yield Him praise at all times and under all conditions. He, verily, standeth witness over all things.

We beseech God to extend wide His shadow, that the true 274 believers may hasten thereunto and that His sincere lovers may seek shelter therein. May He bestow upon men blossoms from the bowers of His grace and stars from the horizon of His providence. We pray God, moreover, to graciously aid the King to do His will and pleasure, and to confirm him in that which shall draw him nigh unto the Dayspring of God's most excellent names, so that he may not give countenance to the injustice he witnesseth, may look upon his subjects with the eye of loving-kindness, and shield them from oppression. We further beseech God, exalted be He, to gather all mankind around the Gulf of the Most Great Ocean, an ocean every drop of which proclaimeth that He is the Harbinger of joy unto the world and the Quickener of all its peoples. Praise be to God, the Lord of the Day of Reckoning!

275    And finally We beseech God, exalted be His glory, to enable thee to aid His Faith and turn towards His justice, that thou mayest judge between the people even as thou wouldst judge between thine own kindred, and mayest choose for them that which thou choosest for thine own self. He, verily, is the All-Powerful, the Most Exalted, the Help in Peril, the Self-Subsisting.

276    Thus have We built the Temple with the hands of power and might, could ye but know it. This is the Temple promised unto you in the Book. Draw ye nigh unto it. This is that which profiteth you, could ye but comprehend it. Be fair, O peoples of the earth! Which is preferable, this, or a temple which is built of clay? Set your faces towards it. Thus have ye been commanded by God, the Help in Peril, the Self-Subsisting. Follow ye His bidding, and praise ye God, your Lord, for that which He hath bestowed upon you. He, verily, is the Truth. No God is there but He. He revealeth what He pleaseth, through His words "Be and it is."

# SÚRIY-I-RA'ÍS

## IN HIS NAME, THE ALL-GLORIOUS!

EARKEN, O CHIEF,[49] to the voice of God, the Sovereign, the Help in Peril, the Self-Subsisting. He, verily, calleth aloud between heaven and earth, summoning all mankind unto the scene of transcendent glory. Neither thy grunting, nor the barking of those around thee, nor the opposition of the hosts of the world can withhold the Almighty from achieving His purpose. The whole world hath been set ablaze by the Word of thy Lord, the All-Glorious, a Word softer than the morning breeze. It hath been manifested in the form of the human temple, and through it God hath quickened the souls of the sincere among His servants. In its inner essence, this Word is the living water by which God hath purified the hearts of such as have turned unto Him and forgotten every other mention, and through which He draweth them nigh unto the seat of His mighty Name. We have sprinkled it upon the people of the graves, and lo, they have risen up, with their gaze fixed upon the shining and resplendent Beauty of their Lord. 1

Thou hast, O Chief, committed that which hath caused Muḥammad, the Apostle of God, to lament in the most sublime Paradise. The world hath made thee proud, so much so that thou hast turned away from the Face through 2

*121*

Whose brightness the Concourse on high hath been illumined. Soon thou shalt find thyself in manifest loss! Thou didst conspire with the Persian Ambassador to harm Me, though I had come unto you from the source of majesty and grandeur with a Revelation that hath solaced the eyes of the favored ones of God.

3    By God! This is the Day wherein the undying Fire crieth out from within all created things: "The Best-Beloved of the worlds is come!" And before all things there standeth a Moses, hearkening to the Word of thy Lord, the Almighty, the All-Knowing. Were We to divest Ourself of the mortal raiment which We have worn in consideration of your weakness, all that are in heaven and on earth would offer up their souls for My sake. To this thy Lord Himself doth testify. None, however, can perceive it save those who have detached themselves from all things for love of their Lord, the Almighty, the Most Powerful.

4    Hast thou imagined thyself capable of extinguishing the fire which God hath kindled in the heart of creation? Nay, by Him Who is the Eternal Truth, couldst thou but know it. Rather, on account of what thy hands have wrought, it blazed higher and burned more fiercely. Erelong will it encompass the earth and all that dwell therein. Thus hath it been decreed by God, and the powers of earth and heaven are unable to thwart His purpose.

5    The day is approaching when the Land of Mystery* and what is beside it shall be changed, and shall pass out of the hands of the King, and commotions shall appear, and the voice of lamentation shall be raised, and the evidences of

---

* Adrianople.

mischief shall be revealed on all sides, and confusion shall spread by reason of that which hath befallen these captives at the hands of the hosts of oppression. The course of things shall be altered, and conditions shall wax so grievous, that the very sands on the desolate hills will moan, and the trees on the mountain will weep, and blood will flow out of all things. Then wilt thou behold the people in sore distress.[50]

O Chief! We revealed Ourself unto thee at one time upon Mount Tíná, and at another time upon Mount Zaytá,[51] and yet again in this hallowed Spot. Following, however, thy corrupt inclinations, thou didst fail to respond and wert accounted with the heedless. Consider, then, and call thou to mind the time when Muḥammad came with clear tokens from Him Who is the Almighty, the All-Knowing. The people were wont to pelt Him with stones from hidden places and in the markets, and they rejected the signs of God, thy Lord and the Lord of thy forefathers. The learned also denied Him, as did their followers, and likewise the kings of the earth, as thou hast heard from the tales of old. Among those kings was Chosroes,[52] to whom Muḥammad sent a blessed epistle summoning him unto God and forbidding him from misbelief. Verily, thy Lord knoweth all things. Following the promptings of his evil and corrupt desires, however, Chosroes waxed arrogant before God and tore up the Tablet. He, verily, is accounted among the inmates of the nethermost fire.

Was it in Pharaoh's power to stay the hand of God from exercising His sovereignty when he acted wantonly in the land and was of the transgressors? From within his own house and in spite of his will We brought forth Him Who conversed with God. Well able are We to achieve Our pur-

6

7

pose. Recall, moreover, how Nimrod kindled the fire of impiety that its flames might consume Abraham, the Friend of God; We delivered Him, however, through the power of truth and seized Nimrod with the fury of Our wrath. Say: The Oppressor* put to death the Beloved of the worlds to quench the light of God amongst the people and to debar them from the wellspring of life eternal in the days of thy Lord, the Gracious, the Most Bountiful.

8    We, too, have revealed the Cause of God in His cities and raised aloft His remembrance amidst them that truly believe in Him. Say: This Youth hath come to quicken the world and unite all its peoples. The day is approaching when that which God hath purposed will have prevailed and thou shalt behold the earth transformed into the all-glorious paradise. Thus hath it been inscribed by the Pen of Revelation upon this weighty Tablet.

9    Forsake Thy mention of the Chief, O Pen, and call to remembrance Anís, that intimate of the love of God who severed himself from the wayward and the infidel. He tore the veils asunder in such wise that the inmates of Paradise could hear them being rent. Glorified be God, the Sovereign, the Powerful, the All-Knowing, the All-Wise.

10    O nightingale! Incline thine ear unto the voice of the All-Glorious on this night when armed troops have surrounded Us while We remain in a state of utmost joy. O would that our blood might be shed upon the earth and our bodies cast upon the dust in the path of God! This, indeed, is My desire and the desire of whosoever hath sought Me and attained unto My most wondrous, Mine incomparable Kingdom.

---

* The Sháh of Iran.

Know thou, O servant, that one day, upon awakening, 11
We found the beloved of God at the mercy of Our adversaries. Sentinels were posted at every gate and no one was
permitted to enter or leave. Indeed, they perpetrated a sore
injustice, for the loved ones of God and His kindred were
left on the first night without food. Such was the fate of
those for whose sake the world and all that is therein have
been created. Woe betide the perpetrators and those who led
them into such evil! Erelong will God consume their souls in
the fire. He, verily, is the fiercest of avengers.

The people surrounded the house, and Muslims and 12
Christians wept over Us, and the voice of lamentation was
upraised between earth and heaven by reason of what the
hands of the oppressors had wrought. We perceived that the
weeping of the people of the Son exceeded the weeping of
others—a sign for such as ponder.

One of My companions offered up his life, cutting his 13
throat with his own hands for the love of God, an act
unheard of in bygone centuries and which God hath set
apart for this Revelation as an evidence of the power of His
might.[53] He, verily, is the Unconstrained, the All-Subduing.
As for the one who thus slew himself in 'Iráq,[54] he truly is
the King and Beloved of Martyrs, and that which he evinced
was a testimony from God unto the peoples of the earth.
Such souls have been influenced by the Word of God, have
tasted the sweetness of His remembrance, and are so trans-
ported by the breezes of reunion that they have detached
themselves from all that dwell on earth and turned unto the
Divine Countenance with faces beaming with light. And
though they have committed an act which God hath forbidden, He hath nevertheless forgiven them as a token of

His mercy. He, verily, is the Ever-Forgiving, the Most Compassionate. So enraptured were these souls by Him Who is the All-Compelling that the reins of volition slipped from their grasp, until at last they ascended to the dwelling of the Unseen and entered the presence of God, the Almighty, the All-Knowing.

14    Say: This Youth hath departed out of this country and deposited beneath every tree and every stone a trust, which God will erelong bring forth through the power of truth. Thus hath the True One come and the command of Him Who is the Ordainer, the All-Wise, been fulfilled. The hosts of earth and heaven are powerless to resist His Cause, nor can all the kings and rulers of the world ever frustrate His purpose. Say: Adversity is the oil which feedeth the flame of this Lamp and by which its light is increased, did ye but know. Indeed, the repudiation of the froward serveth but to proclaim this Faith and to spread the Cause of God and His Revelation throughout the world.

15    Great is your blessedness, inasmuch as ye have forsaken your homes and wandered the land for the love of your Lord, the Almighty, the Ancient of Days, until ye entered the Land of Mystery at a time when the fire of oppression was ablaze and the croaking of the raven of discord had been raised. Ye are My partners in My tribulations, for ye were present with Us during the darksome night in which the hearts of those who testify to the unity of God were agitated. Ye entered this land for the sake of Our love, and departed therefrom through Our command. By the righteousness of God! Because of you the earth itself glorieth over heaven. How excellent is this most sublime, this glorious and exalted bounty! Ye have been deprived of your nest, O birds of

eternity, for the sake of your Lord, the Unconstrained, but your true abode is beneath the wings of the grace of the All-Merciful. Blessed are they that understand.

O My Dhabíh!* May the breaths of the spirit waft upon thee and upon such as have sought communion with thee, inhaled from thee the sweet fragrance of My presence, and hearkened unto that whereby the hearts of the true seekers are sanctified. Render thanks unto God inasmuch as thou hast attained unto the shores of this Most Great Ocean, and give ear to the very atoms of the earth proclaiming: "This is the Best-Beloved of the worlds!" The dwellers of the earth have wronged Him and failed to recognize the One Whose name they ceaselessly invoke. Lost are such as have remained heedless and have opposed Him for Whose loved ones it would have behooved them to offer up their lives, how much more for His own luminous and resplendent Beauty!

Be thou patient, though thy heart be consumed in its separation from God, for He hath granted thee an exalted station in His presence. Nay, thou art even now standing before His face, and We are imparting unto thee, through the tongue of might and power, such words as even the ears of the sincere ones have been deprived of hearing. Say: Were He to utter but one word, that word alone would exceed in sweetness all the sayings of men.

Had Muḥammad, the Apostle of God, attained this Day, He would have exclaimed: "I have truly recognized Thee, O Thou the Desire of the Divine Messengers!" Had Abraham attained it, He too, falling prostrate upon the ground, and in the utmost lowliness before the Lord thy God, would

---

* Dhabíh, meaning literally "sacrifice," refers to Siyyid Ismá'íl of Zavárih.

have cried: "Mine heart is filled with peace, O Thou Lord of all that is in heaven and on earth! I testify that Thou hast unveiled before mine eyes all the glory of Thy power and the full majesty of Thy law! I bear witness, moreover, that through Thy Revelation the hearts of the faithful are well assured and contented." Had Moses Himself attained it, He, likewise, would have raised His voice saying: "All praise be to Thee for having lifted upon me the light of Thy countenance and enrolled me among them that have been privileged to behold Thy face!"

19     Consider the people and their condition. Reflect upon the things that their mouths have uttered and that their hands have wrought in this blessed, this most holy and peerless Day. They that have tarnished the good name of the Cause of God and turned unto the Evil One are accursed of all created things and are numbered among the inmates of the fire. Verily, whosoever hath hearkened to My call shall remain unperturbed by the clamor of all that are on earth; and whosoever is influenced by the words of anyone beside Me hath never heard My call. By God! Such a man is deprived of entering My Kingdom, is debarred from My realms of majesty and power, and is of them that are in utter loss.

20     Sorrow not for that which hath befallen thee. Thou hast borne for My love that which most people have never endured. Thy Lord knoweth and is informed of all. He was with thee in the assemblages and gatherings, and heard that which flowed from the wellspring of thy heart in remembrance of thy Lord, the All-Merciful. This, indeed, is a token of His bountiful favor.

21     Erelong will God raise up from among the kings one who will aid His loved ones. He, verily, encompasseth all things.

He will instill in the hearts the love of His loved ones. This, indeed, is irrevocably decreed by One Who is the Almighty, the Beneficent.

We beseech God to gladden the hearts of His servants 22 through thy call, to make thee an ensign of guidance in His lands, and to assist through thee those who have been brought low. Heed not the one who raised a loud clamor and he who raiseth it even now. Let thy Lord, the Ever-Forgiving, the Most Generous, be all-sufficient unto thee. Relate unto My loved ones that which thou hast seen and learned of the tale of this Youth, and convey unto them that which We have imparted unto thee. Verily, thy Lord assisteth and watcheth over thee at all times and under all conditions. The blessings of the Concourse on high surround thee, and the kindred and the leaves of the holy family who circle round the celestial Tree extol thee with a wondrous praise.

O Pen of Revelation! Call Thou to remembrance him* 23 whose letter reached Us during this darksome night. He it is who wandered from region to region until he entered the City,** seeking the shelter of the mercy of his Lord, the Almighty, the Most High. Eagerly awaiting the favors of his Lord, he dwelt therein for a night, but departed therefrom the following morning as bidden by God, filling with sorrow the heart of this Youth. To this the Almighty is Himself a witness.

Great is thy blessedness, for thou hast received the wine 24 of utterance from the hand of the All-Merciful, and became

---

* Anís.
** Adrianople.

129

so enraptured by the sweet fragrance of the Best-Beloved as to renounce thy comfort and to be numbered with them that have hastened unto His Paradise, the Dawning-Place of the signs of thy Lord, the Gracious, the Peerless. Happy the one who hath quaffed the wine of inner mysteries from the countenance of his Lord and been intoxicated by this pure and crystal draft. By God! It causeth every true believer to soar in the heaven of majesty and grandeur, and transmuteth every doubt into certainty.

25     Grieve not at what hath befallen thee, but put thy whole trust in God, the Almighty, the All-Knowing, the Wise. Raise thy house upon the solid foundation of divine utterances, and give praise to thy Lord. He, verily, shall suffice thee above all the peoples of the earth.

26     God hath, in truth, inscribed your names upon a Tablet wherein are enshrined the hidden secrets of all that hath been. Erelong shall the faithful call to remembrance your exile and all your journeys in His path. He, verily, loveth those who love Him, and is the helper of the sincere. By the righteousness of God! The eyes of the Concourse on high are fixed upon you and their fingers point towards you. Thus doth the bounty of your Lord encompass you. Would that the people might recognize that which hath escaped them in the days of God, the All-Glorious, the All-Praised.

27     Render thanks unto God for having aided thee to know Him and to enter within the precincts of His court at a time when the ungodly surrounded the family of thy Lord and His loved ones, and expelled them from their homes with manifest cruelty, intending to separate us at the shore of the sea. Verily, thy Lord is aware of that which lieth concealed within the breasts of the unbelievers. Say: Even should ye

tear our bodies asunder, ye could not banish from our hearts the love of God. We were of a truth created for sacrifice, and in this do we take pride before all creation.

O thou who art set aglow with the fire of the love of God! Know thou that thy letter hath reached Us and that We have been apprised of its contents. We beseech God to confirm thee in His love and in His good pleasure, to assist thee in the promotion of His Cause, and to number thee with such as have arisen for the triumph of His Faith. 28

As to thy question regarding the soul: Know thou that among the people there are numerous treatises and manifold views as to its stations. Among these are the soul of the kingdom, the soul of the dominion, the celestial soul, the divine soul, the sanctified soul, as well as the benevolent soul, the contented soul, the soul pleasing unto God, the inspired soul, the irascible soul, and the concupiscent soul. Every group hath its own pronouncements concerning the soul and We are disinclined to dwell upon the sayings of the past. Verily, with thy Lord is the knowledge of the former and latter generations. 29

Would that thou wert present before Our throne to hear from the Tongue of Grandeur itself that which thou desirest and scale the loftiest heights of knowledge by the grace of Him Who is the All-Knowing, the All-Wise! The ungodly, however, have intervened between us. Take heed lest thou be grieved thereby. Be content with that which hath been ordained by an irrevocable decree, and be of them that endure with patience. 30

Know that the soul which is common to all men cometh forth following the commingling of things and after their maturation, as thou dost observe in the germ: once it hath 31 developed to its predestined stage, God manifesteth the soul that was latent within it. Thy Lord, verily, doeth what He willeth and ordaineth what He pleaseth.

32    As to the soul which is intended, in truth it hath been called forth by the Word of God and is such that, if it be kindled with the fire of the love of its Lord, neither the waters of opposition nor the oceans of the world can quench its flame. That soul is indeed a fire ablaze in the tree of man which proclaimeth: "No God is there but Him!" Whosoever hearkeneth unto its call is verily of those who have attained unto Him. And when it casteth off its earthly frame, God shall raise it up again in the most excellent of forms and cause it to enter a sublime paradise. Thy Lord, of a certainty, hath power over all things.

33    Know, furthermore, that the life of man proceedeth from the spirit, and the spirit turneth to wheresoever the soul directeth it. Ponder upon that which We have revealed unto thee that thou mayest recognize the Soul of God which hath appeared above the Dayspring of bounty invested with manifest sovereignty.

34    Know also that the soul is endowed with two wings: should it soar in the atmosphere of love and contentment, then it will be related to the All-Merciful. And should it fly in the atmosphere of self and desire, then it will pertain to the Evil One; may God shield and protect us and protect you therefrom, O ye who perceive! Should the soul become ignited with the fire of the love of God, it is called benevolent and pleasing unto God, but should it be consumed with the fire of passion, it is known as the concupiscent soul. Thus have We expounded this subject for thee that thou mayest obtain a clear understanding.

O Pen of the Most High! Recount unto him who hath  35
turned unto Thy Lord, the All-Glorious, that which shall
enable him to dispense with the sayings of men. Say: Spirit,
mind, soul, and the powers of sight and hearing are but
one single reality which hath manifold expressions owing to
the diversity of its instruments. As thou dost observe, man's
power to comprehend, move, speak, hear, and see all derive
from this sign of his Lord within him. It is single in its essence, yet manifold through the diversity of its instruments.
This, verily, is a certain truth. For example, if it directeth
its attention to the means of hearing, then hearing and its
attributes become manifest. Likewise, if it directeth itself to
the means of vision, a different effect and attribute appear.
Reflect upon this subject that thou mayest comprehend
the true meaning of what hath been intended, find thyself
independent of the sayings of the people, and be of them
that are well assured. In like manner, when this sign of God
turneth towards the brain, the head, and such means, the
powers of the mind and the soul are manifested. Thy Lord,
verily, is potent to do whatsoever He pleaseth.

All that We have mentioned here hath been elucidated  36
in the Tablets We have revealed in response to questions
regarding the disconnected letters of the Qur'án. Ponder
them that thou mayest comprehend that which hath been
sent down from the Kingdom of Him Who is the Almighty,
the All-Praised. Thus have We chosen to be concise in this
Tablet. We beseech God to acquaint thee through this brief
exposition with that which words can never hope to exhaust,
and to give thee to drink of the limitless oceans from this
cup. Thy Lord, verily, is the All-Bountiful and unassailable
in His power.

37      O Pen of the Ancient of Days! Call Thou to remembrance 'Alí,* he who sojourned with Thee in 'Iráq until the Daystar of the world departed therefrom. He forsook his home to attain the court of Thy presence at a time when We were captive in the hands of such as have been deprived of the sweet savors of the All-Merciful. Grieve not at what hath befallen Us and thee in the path of God. Rest assured and persevere. He, verily, rendereth victorious those who love Him, and His might is equal to all things. Whoso turneth unto Him brighteneth thereby the faces of the Concourse on high, and unto this God Himself is My witness.

38      Say: O people, do ye imagine that, after rejecting the One through Whom the religions of the world have been made manifest, ye still bear allegiance to the Faith of God? By the righteousness of God! Ye are accounted among the inmates of the Fire. Thus hath the decree been recorded in the Tablets by the Pen of God. Say: Never will the barking of dogs deter the Nightingale from warbling its melodies. Ponder awhile that perchance ye may discover a path leading to the Eternal Truth.

39      Say: Magnified art Thou, O Lord my God! I entreat Thee by the tears Thy lovers have shed in their longing after Thee, and by the yearning of those who cry out in their separation from Thee, and by Thy Best-Beloved Who hath fallen into the hands of Thine adversaries, to graciously assist those who have sought refuge beneath the sheltering wings of Thy favor and loving-kindness, and who have yearned for no other Lord except Thee.

---

* Mírzá 'Alí-Akbar-i-Naráqí.

We have forsaken our homes, O Lord, in our eagerness 40
to meet Thee and in our longing to be united with Thee.
We have traversed land and sea to attain the court of Thy
presence and to give ear to Thy verses. When we arrived
at the shores of the sea, however, we were held back from
Thee, as the ungodly intervened between us and the light of
Thy countenance.

O Lord! Dire thirst hath seized us, and with Thee are the 41
soft-flowing waters of eternal life. Potent art Thou to do
what pleaseth Thee. Deny us not the object of our quest.
Write down then for us the recompense decreed for such of
Thy servants as enjoy near access to Thee and are wholly
devoted to Thy will. Make us so steadfast in Thy love that
naught shall keep us back from Thee or deter us from Thine
adoration. Powerful art Thou to do Thy pleasure. Thou,
verily, art the Almighty, the Most Generous.

# LAWḤ-I-RA'ÍS

# HE IS IN HIS OWN RIGHT
# THE SUPREME RULER!

T HE PEN OF THE MOST HIGH PROCLAIMETH: O thou who 1
hast imagined thyself to be the most exalted of men[55]
and who hast regarded as the lowliest of all creatures this
divine Youth, through Whom the eyes of the Concourse
on high have been illumined and made radiant! This Youth
hath sought nothing from thee or from such as are like unto
thee, inasmuch as from time immemorial, whenever the
Manifestations of the All-Merciful and the Exponents of
His unfading glory have stepped out of the Realm of eternity into this mortal world and revealed themselves to revive
the dead, men such as thee have considered these sanctified
Souls and Temples of Divine Oneness, upon Whom must
needs depend the rehabilitation of the peoples of the earth,
to be stirrers of mischief and worthy of blame. These men,
verily, have all returned unto dust. Thou, too, shalt erelong
take abode therein and find thyself in grievous loss.

Even if this Lifegiver and World Reformer be in thine 2
estimation guilty of sedition and strife, what crime could
have been committed by a group of women, children, and
suckling mothers that they should be thus afflicted with the
scourge of thine anger and wrath? No faith or religion hath
ever held children responsible. The Pen of divine Command

hath exempted them, yet the fire of thy tyranny and oppression encompasseth all. If thou bearest allegiance to any faith or religion, then thou shouldst know that, according to all the heavenly Books and all the divinely inspired and weighty Scriptures, children are not to be held accountable. Aside from this, not even those who disbelieve in God have perpetrated such unseemly acts. Since from every thing an effect becometh manifest, a fact that none can deny save those who are bereft of reason and understanding, it is certain that the sighs of these children and the cries of these wronged ones will have their due consequence.

3    Ye have plundered and unjustly despoiled a group of people who have never rebelled in your domains, nor disobeyed your government, but rather kept to themselves and engaged day and night in the remembrance of God. Later, when the order was issued to banish this Youth, all were filled with dismay. The officials in charge of My expulsion declared, however: "These others have not been charged with any offense and have not been expelled by the government. Should they desire to accompany you, no one will oppose them." These hapless souls therefore paid their own expenses, forsook all their possessions, and, contenting themselves with Our presence and placing their whole trust in God, journeyed once again with Him until the fortress of 'Akká became the prison of Bahá.

4    Upon our arrival, we were surrounded by guards and confined together, men and women, young and old alike, in the army barracks. The first night all were deprived of either food or drink, for the sentries were guarding the gate of the barracks and permitted no one to leave. No one gave a thought to the plight of these wronged ones. They even begged for water, and were refused.

Time hath passed, and we all remain confined in these    5
barracks, notwithstanding that during the five years we
dwelt in Adrianople, all its inhabitants, whether learned or
ignorant, rich or poor, bore witness to the purity and sanctity of these servants. At the time this Youth was departing
from Adrianople, one of the loved ones of God attempted
to take his own life, so unbearable to him was the sight of
this Wronged One in the hands of His oppressors. During
the journey we were thrice compelled to change ships, and it
is evident how much the children suffered as a result. Upon
disembarking, four of the believers were separated and prevented from accompanying Us. As this Youth was leaving,
one of the four, named 'Abdu'l-Ghaffár, cast himself into
the sea, and no one knoweth what befell him thereafter.[56]

All this is but a drop in the ocean of the wrongs that    6
have been inflicted upon Us, and still ye are not satisfied!
The officials enforce every day a new decree, and no end
is in sight to their tyranny. Night and day they conceive
new schemes. They have assigned each prisoner, from the
government storehouse, a daily allowance of three loaves of
bread that no one can eat. From the foundation of the world
until the present day a cruelty such as this hath neither been
seen nor heard of.

By the righteousness of Him Who hath caused Bahá to    7
speak forth before all that are in heaven and all that are on
earth! Ye have neither rank nor mention among them that
have offered up their souls, their bodies and their substance
for the love of God, the All-Powerful, the All-Compelling,
the Almighty. A handful of clay is greater in the sight of
God than all your dominion and your sovereignty, and all
your might and your fortune. Should it be His wish, He
would scatter you in dust. Soon will He seize you in His

wrathful anger, and sedition will be stirred up in your midst, and your dominions will be disrupted. Then will ye bewail and lament, and will find none to help or succor you.

8  In making mention of these matters, it is not Our purpose to rouse you from your slumber, since the fury of God's wrath hath so encompassed you that ye shall never take heed. Nor is it Our intention to recount the iniquities visited upon these pure and blessed souls, for they have been so intoxicated with the wine of the All-Merciful and are so carried away with the inebriating effect of the living waters of His loving providence that even were they to suffer all the cruelties of the world for His sake, they would remain content and yield thanks unto Him. These souls have never held, nor shall they ever hold any grievance. Nay, their blood continually imploreth and beseecheth the Lord of the worlds that it might be spilt upon the dust in His path, and their heads yearn to be borne aloft on spears for the sake of the Beloved of hearts and souls.

9  Several times calamities have overtaken you, and yet ye failed utterly to take heed. One of them was the conflagration which devoured most of the City[57] with the flames of justice, and concerning which many poems were written, stating that no such fire had ever been witnessed. And yet, ye waxed more heedless. Plague, likewise, broke out, and ye still failed to give heed! Be expectant, however, for the wrath of God is ready to overtake you. Erelong will ye behold that which hath been sent down from the Pen of My command.

10  Have ye fondly imagined your glory to be imperishable and your dominion to be everlasting? Nay, by Him Who is the All-Merciful! Neither will your glory last, nor will Mine abasement endure. Such abasement, in the estimation of a true man, is the pride of every glory.

When I was still a child and had not yet attained the age     11
of maturity, My father made arrangements in Ṭihrán for
the marriage of one of My older brothers, and as is cus-
tomary in that city, the festivities lasted for seven days and
seven nights. On the last day it was announced that the play
"Sháh Sulṭán Salím" would be presented. A large number
of princes, dignitaries, and notables of the capital gathered
for the occasion. I was sitting in one of the upper rooms
of the building and observing the scene. Presently a tent
was pitched in the courtyard, and before long some small
human-like figures, each appearing to be no more than
about a hand's span in height, were seen to emerge from it
and raise the call: "His Majesty is coming! Arrange the seats
at once!" Other figures then came forth, some of whom were
seen to be engaged in sweeping, others in sprinkling water,
and thereafter another, who was announced as the chief
town crier, raised his call and bade the people assemble for
an audience with the king. Next, several groups of figures
made their appearance and took their places, the first at-
tired in hats and sashes after the Persian fashion, the second
wielding battleaxes, and the third comprising a number of
footmen and executioners carrying bastinados. Finally there
appeared, arrayed in regal majesty and crowned with a royal
diadem, a kingly figure, bearing himself with the utmost
haughtiness and grandeur, at turns advancing and pausing
in his progress, who proceeded with great solemnity, poise
and dignity to seat himself upon his throne.

At that moment a volley of shots was fired, a fanfare of     12
trumpets was sounded, and king and tent were enveloped in
a pall of smoke. When it had cleared, the king, ensconced
upon his throne, was seen surrounded by a suite of ministers, princes, and dignitaries of state who, having taken

their places, were standing at attention in his presence. A captured thief was then brought before the king, who gave the order that the offender should be beheaded. Without a moment's delay the chief executioner cut off the thief's head, whence a blood-like liquid came forth. After this the king held audience with his court, during which intelligence was received that a rebellion had broken out on a certain frontier. Thereupon the king reviewed his troops and dispatched several regiments supported by artillery to quell the uprising. A few moments later cannons were heard booming from behind the tent, and it was announced that a battle had been engaged.

13    This Youth regarded the scene with great amazement. When the royal audience was ended, the curtain was drawn, and, after some twenty minutes, a man emerged from behind the tent carrying a box under his arm.

14    "What is this box," I asked him, "and what was the nature of this display?"

15    "All this lavish display and these elaborate devices," he replied, "the king, the princes, and the ministers, their pomp and glory, their might and power, everything you saw, are now contained within this box."

16    I swear by My Lord Who, through a single word of His Mouth, hath brought into being all created things! Ever since that day, all the trappings of the world have seemed in the eyes of this Youth akin to that same spectacle. They have never been, nor will they ever be, of any weight and consequence, be it to the extent of a grain of mustard seed. How greatly I marveled that men should pride themselves upon such vanities, whilst those possessed of insight, ere they witness any evidence of human glory, perceive with certainty

the inevitability of its waning. "Never have I looked upon any thing save that I have seen extinction before it; and God, verily, is a sufficient witness!"

It behooveth everyone to traverse this brief span of life 17 with sincerity and fairness. Should one fail to attain unto the recognition of Him Who is the Eternal Truth, let him at least conduct himself with reason and justice. Erelong these outward trappings, these visible treasures, these earthly vanities, these arrayed armies, these adorned vestures, these proud and overweening souls, all shall pass into the confines of the grave, as though into that box. In the eyes of those possessed of insight, all this conflict, contention and vain-glory hath ever been, and will ever be, like unto the play and pastimes of children. Take heed, and be not of them that see and yet deny.

Our call concerneth not this Youth and the loved ones 18 of God, for they are already sore-tried and imprisoned and expect nothing from men such as thee. Our purpose is that thou mayest lift up thy head from the couch of heedlessness, shake off the slumber of negligence, and cease to oppose unjustly the servants of God. So long as thy power and ascendancy endure, strive to alleviate the suffering of the oppressed. Shouldst thou judge with fairness and observe with the eye of discernment the conflicts and pursuits of this transient world, thou wouldst readily acknowledge that they are even as the play which We have described.

Hearken unto the words of the one true God and pride 19 thyself not in the things of this world. What hath become of those like unto thee who falsely claimed lordship on earth, who sought to quench the light of God in His land and to destroy the foundation of His mighty edifice in His cities?

Where are they to be seen now? Be fair in thy judgment and return unto God, that perchance He might cancel the trespasses of thy vain life. Alas, We know that thou shalt never attain unto this, for such is thy cruelty that it hath made hell to blaze and the Spirit to lament, and hath caused the pillars of the Throne to shake and the hearts of the faithful to tremble.

20     O peoples of the earth! Incline your inner ears to the call of this Wronged One and pause to reflect upon the story that We have recounted. Perchance ye may not be consumed by the fire of self and passion, nor allow the vain and worthless objects of this nether world to withhold you from Him Who is the Eternal Truth. Glory and abasement, riches and poverty, tranquillity and tribulation, all will pass away, and all the peoples of the earth will erelong be laid to rest in their tombs. It behooveth therefore every man of insight to fix his gaze upon the goal of eternity, that perchance by the grace of Him Who is the Ancient King he may attain unto the immortal Kingdom and abide beneath the shade of the Tree of His Revelation.

21     Though this world be fraught with deception and deceit, yet it continually warneth all men of their impending extinction. The death of the father proclaimeth to the son that he, too, shall pass away. Would that the inhabitants of the world who have amassed riches for themselves and have strayed far from the True One might know who will eventually lay hand on their treasures; but, by the life of Bahá, no one knoweth this save God, exalted be His glory.

22     The poet Saná'í, may God's mercy rest upon him, hath said: "Take heed, O ye whose unseemly conduct hath darkened your faces! Take heed, O ye whose beards have been

whitened by age!" Alas, most of the people are fast asleep. They are even as the man who, in his drunkenness, became attracted to a dog, took it in his embrace, and made it his plaything, and who, when the morn of discernment dawned and the light of the sun enveloped the horizon, realized that the object of his affection was but a dog. Then, filled with shame and remorse, he repaired to his abode.

Think not that thou hast abased this Youth or prevailed over Him. The least of creatures ruleth over thee, and yet thou perceivest not. The lowliest and most abject of all things holdeth sway over thee, and that is none other than self and passion, which have ever been reprehensible. Were it not for God's consummate wisdom, thou wouldst have been able to plainly behold thine own helplessness and that of all who dwell on earth. Our abasement is indeed the glory of His Cause, could ye but understand. 23

This Youth hath ever been disinclined to breathe a word contrary to courtesy, for courtesy is Our raiment, wherewith We have adorned the temples of Our well-favored servants. Otherwise, some of the deeds that ye believe to be concealed would have been divulged in this Tablet. 24

O exponent of might and power! These young children and these poor ones in God did not need to be accompanied by officers and soldiers. Upon our arrival in Gallipoli, a major by the name of 'Umar came into Our presence. God is well aware of what he said. After some exchanges in which his own innocence and thy guilt were mentioned, We declared: "From the outset, a gathering should have been convened at which the learned men of this age could have met with this Youth in order to determine what offense these servants have committed. But now the matter hath gone be- 25 yond such considerations, and, according to thine own assertion, thou art charged with incarcerating Us in the most desolate of cities. There is a matter, which, if thou findest it possible, I request thee to submit to His Majesty the Sultán, that for ten minutes this Youth be enabled to meet him, so that he may demand whatsoever he deemeth as a sufficient testimony and regardeth as proof of the veracity of Him Who is the Truth. Should God enable Him to produce it, let him, then, release these wronged ones, and leave them to themselves."

26    He promised to transmit this message, and to give Us his reply. We received, however, no news from him. Although it becometh not Him Who is the Truth to present Himself before any person, inasmuch as all have been created to obey Him, yet in view of the condition of these little children and the large number of women so far removed from their friends and countries, We have acquiesced in this matter. In spite of this nothing hath resulted. 'Umar himself is alive and accessible. Inquire from him, that the truth may be made known unto you.

27    Most of Our companions now lie sick in this prison, and none knoweth what befell Us, except God, the Almighty, the All-Knowing. In the days following Our arrival, two of these servants hastened to the realms above. For an entire day the guards insisted that, until they were paid for the shrouds and burial, those blessed bodies could not be removed, although no one had requested any help from them. At that time we were devoid of earthly means, and pleaded that they leave the matter unto us and allow those present to carry the bodies, but they refused. Finally, a carpet was taken to the bazaar to be sold, and the sum obtained was

delivered to the guards. Later, it was learned that they had merely dug a shallow grave into which they had placed both blessed bodies, although they had taken twice the amount required for shrouds and burial.

The pen is powerless to depict and the tongue faileth to describe the trials which We have suffered. Yet sweeter than honey to Me is the bitterness of such tribulations. Would that at every instant all the afflictions of the world could, in the path of God and for the sake of His love, be visited upon this evanescent Soul Who is immersed in the ocean of divine knowledge! 28

We implore God for patience and forbearance, inasmuch as thou art but a feeble creature and bereft of comprehension. Wert thou to awaken and inhale the fragrance of the breezes that waft from the retreats of eternity, thou wouldst readily abandon all that thou dost possess and in which thou dost rejoice, and choose to abide in one of the dilapidated rooms of this Most Great Prison. Beseech God to grant thee such mature understanding as to enable thee to distinguish praiseworthy actions from those which merit blame. Peace be upon him who followeth the way of guidance! 29

# LAWḤ-I-FU'ÁD

# HE IS THE MOST HOLY, THE MOST GLORIOUS!

KÁF. ẒÁ'.[58] We call unto thee from beyond the sea of grandeur, upon the crimson land, above the horizon of tribulation. Verily, no God is there save Him, the Almighty, the Most Generous. Walk thou steadfastly in My Cause and follow not the ways of those who, upon attaining unto the object of their desire, denied God, the Lord of Lords. Erelong shall He lay hold upon them in His wrath, and He, verily, is the All-Powerful, the All-Subduing.

Know thou that, through the power of His sovereign might, God hath seized him who was the foremost amongst them that passed judgment against Us. When he saw his torment approaching, he fled to Paris to seek recourse to physicians.

"Is there none to help me?" he asked.

He was smitten upon the mouth and told: "There is no escape!"[59]

And when he turned towards the angel of wrath, he well-nigh expired from fear. "I have a house full of riches," he pleaded. "I have a palace on the Bosphorus, beneath which the rivers flow."

The angel replied: "No ransom shall be accepted from thee on this day, even shouldst thou offer up all things visible and invisible. Hearest thou not the sighs of the kindred of God, whom thou didst cast into prison without proof or testimony? Thy deed hath provoked the lamentation of the inmates of Paradise, and of those who circle morn and eve round the Throne on high. The wrath of thy Lord hath descended upon thee, and stern is He in His chastisement!"[60]

7   He made reply: "I held command over the people, and here is the mandate of my authority."

8   "Hold thy peace, O denier of the Day of Judgment!"[61]

9   He implored: "Is no respite possible so that I may send for my family?"

10  "Far from it, O disbeliever in the verses of God!"

11  Thereupon the keepers of the fathomless abyss called unto him: "The gates of Hell have opened wide to receive thee, O thou who hast turned away from thy Lord, the Unconstrained! Repair unto its fire, for it yearneth after thee. Hast thou forgotten, O rejected one, when thou wert the Nimrod of the age, how thy tyranny eclipsed the very cruelties of Pharaoh, the Lord of the Stakes?[62] By God! Thine iniquity hath rent asunder the veil of sanctity and caused the pillars of heaven to tremble. Where canst thou find refuge now? Who shall protect thee from the dreadful scourge of thy Lord, the All-Compelling? There is no haven for thee in this Day, O ungodly doubter!" Whereupon the agony of death seized him and he saw no more. Thus did We lay hold on him in Our wrathful anger, and severe is thy Lord in His punishment.

12  Then an angel from the right hand of the Throne summoned him: "Behold the angel of affliction. Is there any place to flee to save hell, wherein the heart[63] boileth?" And the angel of chastisement received his spirit, and a voice proclaimed: "Enter the bottomless pit which hath been

promised in the Book, and whose existence thou didst day and night deny!"

Soon will We dismiss the one who was like unto him,* and will lay hold on their Chief who ruleth the land,** and I, verily, am the Almighty, the All-Compelling. Be thou steadfast in the Cause of God and extol thy Lord morn and eve. Suffer not the light of thy soul to be quenched by the calumnies of the one who was so blinded by Our bestowals as to turn away from God, the Lord of all names. He inspireth his devoted followers even as the Evil One prompteth his own. Erelong shalt thou behold him in evident loss both in this world and in the world to come. He, indeed, is among those whom an afflictive torment doth await. He dispatched an epistle to someone in that land, a writ of the workers of iniquity, in which he mocked God and recorded that which filled all created things with dismay. Say: Canst thou find anyone to protect thee when the wrath of God, the All-Powerful, the Unconstrained, is visited upon thee? 13

Thus have We informed thee of that which lieth concealed within the hearts of men. Verily, thy Lord is the Almighty, the All-Knowing. Arise for the triumph of this Cause, and gather together My loved ones. Help them to see the truth in this Day when the feet of men have slipped. Say: It behooveth every true believer to assist his Lord. He, verily, is your helper, while the people have no one to turn to in this Day. 14

---

* 'Alí Páshá.
** Sulṭán 'Abdu'l-'Azíz.

15    Then We seized Mihdí,<sup>64</sup> to whom We had promised divine chastisement in Our Books and Scriptures. When Our awful majesty encompassed him, he entreated: "May I not retrace my steps?"

16    A voice exclaimed: "Woe betide thee, O disbeliever in the Day of Resurrection! This is the nethermost fire, and its flames have been made to blaze for thee. Thou didst forsake all righteous deeds in thy vain and futile life, and now thou hast none to shield thee from God. Thou art indeed he who caused all hearts to be consumed and the Holy Spirit to lament."

17    He pleaded: "Is there yet no refuge for me?"

18    "Nay, by my Lord, even shouldst thou seek recourse to every possible means!"

19    Thereupon he cried out in such distress as to cause the people of the graves to tremble, and was seized by the Hand of invincible power. A voice then proclaimed: "Return unto the seat of wrath in the fire of hell; wretched and evil be thine abode!"

20    Thus did We lay hold on him as We laid hold on those who preceded him. Behold their houses which We have left to the spiders, and take heed, O ye who are endued with understanding! He it is who opposed God, and for whom the verses of wrath were revealed in the Book. Blessed is he who readeth it and pondereth its contents, for a goodly end doth in truth await him.

21    Thus have We recounted unto thee the tale of the evildoers, that thine eyes may be solaced. As for thee, there lieth in store naught but a blissful end.

# SÚRIY-I-MULÚK

## HE IS THE ALMIGHTY!

THIS IS A TABLET FROM THIS SERVANT, who is called Ḥusayn in the kingdom of names, to the concourse of the kings of the earth. Haply they may approach it in a spirit of open-mindedness, discover from its message the mysteries of divine providence, and be of those that comprehend its meaning, and perchance they may forsake all they possess, turn towards the retreats of holiness, and draw nigh unto God, the All-Glorious, the Incomparable.

O kings of the earth! Give ear unto the Voice of God, calling from this sublime, this fruit-laden Tree, that hath sprung out of the Crimson Hill, upon the holy Plain, intoning the words: "There is none other God but He, the Mighty, the All-Powerful, the All-Wise." This is a Spot which hath been sanctified by God for those who approach it, a Spot wherein His Voice may be heard from the celestial Tree of Holiness. Fear God, O concourse of kings, and suffer not yourselves to be deprived of this most sublime grace. Fling away, then, the things ye possess, and take fast hold on the Handle of God, the Exalted, the Great. Set your hearts towards the Face of God, and abandon that which your desires have bidden you to follow, and be not of those who perish.

3    Relate unto them, O Servant, the story of 'Alí,* when He came unto them with truth, bearing His glorious and weighty Book, and holding in His hands a testimony and proof from God, and holy and blessed tokens from Him. Ye, however, O kings, have failed to heed the Remembrance of God in His days and to be guided by the lights which arose and shone forth above the horizon of a resplendent Heaven. Ye examined not His Cause when so to do would have been better for you than all that the sun shineth upon, could ye but perceive it. Ye remained careless until the divines of Persia—those cruel ones—pronounced judgment against Him, and unjustly slew Him. His spirit ascended unto God, and the eyes of the inmates of Paradise and the angels that are nigh unto Him wept sore by reason of this cruelty. Beware that ye be not careless henceforth as ye have been careless aforetime. Return, then, unto God, your Maker, and be not of the heedless.

4    Say: The Sun of vicegerency hath dawned, the Point of knowledge and wisdom hath been made plain, and the Testimony of God, the Almighty, the All-Wise, hath been made manifest. Say: The Moon of eternity hath risen in the midmost heaven, and its light hath illumined the dwellers of the realms above. My face hath come forth from the veils, and shed its radiance upon all that is in heaven and on earth; and yet, ye turned not towards Him, notwithstanding that ye were created for Him, O concourse of kings! Follow, therefore, that which I speak unto you, and hearken unto it with your hearts, and be not of such as have turned aside.

---

* The Báb.

For your glory consisteth not in your sovereignty, but rather in your nearness unto God and your observance of His command as sent down in His holy and preserved Tablets. Should any one of you rule over the whole earth, and over all that lieth within it and upon it, its seas, its lands, its mountains, and its plains, and yet be not remembered by God, all these would profit him not, could ye but know it.

Know ye that a servant's glory resideth in his nearness unto God, and that, unless he draweth nigh unto Him, naught else can ever profit him, even should he hold sway over the entire creation. Say: The breeze of God hath wafted over you from the retreats of Paradise, but ye have neglected it and chosen to persist in your waywardness. Guidance hath been given unto you from God, but ye have failed to follow it and preferred to reject its truth. The Lamp of God hath been lit within the niche of His Cause, but ye have neglected to seek the radiance of its glory and to draw nigh unto its light. And still ye slumber upon the couch of heedlessness!

Arise, then, and make steadfast your feet, and make ye amends for that which hath escaped you, and set then yourselves towards His holy Court, on the shore of His mighty Ocean, so that the pearls of knowledge and wisdom, which God hath stored up within the shell of His radiant heart, may be revealed unto you. Such is the counsel that shall profit you most; make of it your provision, that ye may be of those who are guided aright. Beware lest ye hinder the breeze of God from blowing over your hearts, the breeze through which the hearts of such as have turned unto Him can be quickened. Hearken unto the clear admonitions that We have revealed for you in this Tablet, that God, in turn, may hearken unto you, and may open before your faces the portals of His mercy. He, verily, is the Compassionate, the Merciful.

7    Lay not aside the fear of God, O kings of the earth, and beware that ye transgress not the bounds which the Almighty hath fixed. Observe the injunctions laid upon you in His Book, and take good heed not to overstep their limits. Be vigilant, that ye may not do injustice to anyone, be it to the extent of a grain of mustard seed. Tread ye the path of justice, for this, verily, is the straight path.

8    Compose your differences and reduce your armaments, that the burden of your expenditures may be lightened, and that your minds and hearts may be tranquilized. Heal the dissensions that divide you, and ye will no longer be in need of any armaments except what the protection of your cities and territories demandeth. Fear ye God, and take heed not to outstrip the bounds of moderation and be numbered among the extravagant.

9    We have learned that ye are increasing your outlay every year, and are laying the burden thereof on your subjects. This, verily, is more than they can bear, and is a grievous injustice. Decide justly between men, O kings, and be ye the emblems of justice amongst them. This, if ye judge fairly, is the thing that behooveth you, and beseemeth your station.

10    Beware not to deal unjustly with anyone that appealeth to you and entereth beneath your shadow. Walk ye in the fear of God, and be ye of them that lead a godly life. Rest not on your power, your armies, and treasures. Put your whole trust and confidence in God, Who hath created you, and seek ye His help in all your affairs. Succor cometh from Him alone. He succoreth whom He willeth with the hosts of the heavens and of the earth.

Know ye that the poor are the trust of God in your midst.   11
Watch that ye betray not His trust, that ye deal not unjustly
with them and that ye walk not in the ways of the treacherous. Ye will most certainly be called upon to answer for His
trust on the day when the Balance of Justice shall be set, the
day when unto everyone shall be rendered his due, when the
doings of all men, be they rich or poor, shall be weighed.

If ye pay no heed unto the counsels which, in peerless and   12
unequivocal language, We have revealed in this Tablet, Divine chastisement shall assail you from every direction, and
the sentence of His justice shall be pronounced against you.
On that day ye shall have no power to resist Him, and shall
recognize your own impotence. Have mercy on yourselves
and on those beneath you, and judge ye between them according to the precepts prescribed by God in His most holy
and exalted Tablet, a Tablet wherein He hath assigned to
each and every thing its settled measure, in which He hath
given, with distinctness, an explanation of all things, and
which is in itself a monition unto them that believe in Him.

Examine Our Cause, inquire into the things that have   13
befallen Us, and decide justly between Us and Our enemies,
and be ye of them that act equitably towards their neighbor.
If ye stay not the hand of the oppressor, if ye fail to safeguard
the rights of the downtrodden, what right have ye then to
vaunt yourselves among men? What is it of which ye can
rightly boast? Is it on your food and your drink that ye pride
yourselves, on the riches ye lay up in your treasuries, on the
diversity and the cost of the ornaments with which ye deck
yourselves? If true glory were to consist in the possession
of such perishable things, then the earth on which ye walk
must needs vaunt itself over you, because it supplieth you,

and bestoweth upon you, these very things, by the decree of the Almighty. In its bowels are contained, according to what God hath ordained, all that ye possess. From it, as a sign of His mercy, ye derive your riches. Behold then your state, the thing in which ye glory! Would that ye could perceive it!

14      Nay, by Him Who holdeth in His grasp the kingdom of the entire creation! Nowhere doth your true and abiding glory reside except in your firm adherence unto the precepts of God, your wholehearted observance of His laws, your resolution to see that they do not remain unenforced, and to pursue steadfastly the right course.

15      O kings of Christendom! Heard ye not the saying of Jesus, the Spirit of God, "I go away, and come again unto you"?[65] Wherefore, then, did ye fail, when He did come again unto you in the clouds of heaven, to draw nigh unto Him, that ye might behold His face, and be of them that attained His Presence? In another passage He saith: "When He, the Spirit of Truth, is come, He will guide you into all truth."[66] And yet behold how, when He did bring the truth, ye refused to turn your faces towards Him, and persisted in disporting yourselves with your pastimes and fancies. Ye welcomed Him not, neither did ye seek His Presence, that ye might hear the verses of God from His own mouth, and partake of the manifold wisdom of the Almighty, the All-Glorious, the All-Wise. Ye have, by reason of your failure, hindered the breath of God from being wafted over you, and have withheld from your souls the sweetness of its fragrance. Ye continue roving with delight in the valley of your corrupt desires. By God! Ye, and all ye possess, shall pass away. Ye shall, most certainly, return to God, and shall be called to

account for your doings in the presence of Him Who shall gather together the entire creation.

Again, heard ye not that which hath been recorded in the 16 Gospel concerning those "which were born, not of blood, nor of the will of the flesh, nor of the will of man, but of God"[67]—that is, those who have been made manifest through the power of God? Wherefore it becometh evident that one may well be manifested in the world of creation who is truly of God, the Almighty, the All-Knowing, the All-Wise. How is it then that when word reached you of Our Cause, ye failed to inquire from Our own lips, that ye might distinguish truth from falsehood, discover Our aim and purpose, and learn of the afflictions which We have suffered at the hands of an evil and wayward generation?

O Minister of the King of Paris![68] Hast thou forgotten the 17 pronouncement recorded in the Gospel according to John concerning the Word and those who are its Manifestations? And hast thou ignored the counsels of the Spirit* concerning the Manifestations of the Word, and been numbered with the heedless? If not, wherefore then didst thou conspire with the Minister of Persia[69] to inflict upon Us that which hath caused the hearts of men of insight and understanding to melt, the tears of the denizens of the Realm of eternity to flow, and the souls of them who are nigh unto God to mourn? And all this thou didst commit without seeking to examine Our Cause or to discern its truth. For is it not thy

---

* Jesus.

165

clear duty to investigate this Cause, to inform thyself of the things that have befallen Us, to judge with equity, and to cleave unto justice?

18    Thy days shall pass away, thy ministry shall come to an end, and thy possessions shall vanish and be no more. Then, in the presence of the almighty King, thou shalt be called to answer for that which thy hands have wrought. How many the ministers who came before thee into this world, men who exceeded thee in power, excelled thee in station, and surpassed thee in wealth, and yet returned to dust, leaving upon the face of the earth neither name nor trace, and are now plunged in grievous remorse. Amongst them were those who failed in their duty towards God, followed their own desires, and trod the path of lust and wickedness. And amongst them were those who observed that which hath been prescribed in the verses of God, judged with fairness by the divine guidance that overshadowed them, and entered beneath the shelter of the mercy of their Lord.

19    I admonish thee, and those who are like thee, to deal not with anyone as ye have dealt with Us. Beware lest ye follow in the footsteps of the Evil One and walk in the ways of the unjust. Take from this world only to the measure of your needs, and forgo that which exceedeth them. Observe equity in all your judgments, and transgress not the bounds of justice, nor be of them that stray from its path.

20    Twenty years have passed, O kings, during which We have, each day, tasted the agony of a fresh tribulation. No one of them that were before Us hath endured the things We have endured. Would that ye could perceive it! They that rose up against Us have put us to death, have shed our blood, have plundered our property, and violated our honor.

Though aware of most of our afflictions, ye, nevertheless, have failed to stay the hand of the aggressor. For is it not your clear duty to restrain the tyranny of the oppressor, and to deal equitably with your subjects, that your high sense of justice may be fully demonstrated to all mankind?

God hath committed into your hands the reins of the government of the people, that ye may rule with justice over them, safeguard the rights of the downtrodden, and punish the wrongdoers. If ye neglect the duty prescribed unto you by God in His Book, your names shall be numbered with those of the unjust in His sight. Grievous, indeed, will be your error. Cleave ye to that which your imaginations have devised, and cast behind your backs the commandments of God, the Most Exalted, the Inaccessible, the All-Compelling, the Almighty? Cast away the things ye possess, and cling to that which God hath bidden you observe. Seek ye His grace, for he that seeketh it treadeth His straight Path. 21

Consider the state in which We are, and behold ye the ills and troubles that have tried Us. Neglect Us not, though it be for a moment, and judge ye between Us and Our enemies with equity. This will, surely, be a manifest advantage unto you. Thus do We relate to you Our tale, and recount the things that have befallen Us, that ye might take off Our ills and ease Our burden. Let him who will, relieve Us from Our trouble; and as to him that willeth not, My Lord is assuredly the best of helpers. 22

Warn and acquaint the people, O Servant, with the things We have sent down unto Thee, and let the fear of no one dismay Thee, and be Thou not of them that waver. The day is approaching when God will have exalted His Cause and magnified His testimony in the eyes of all who 23 are in the heavens and all who are on the earth. Place, in all circumstances, Thy whole trust in Thy Lord, and fix Thy gaze upon Him, and turn away from all them that repudiate His truth. Let God, Thy Lord, be Thy sufficing succorer and helper. We have pledged Ourself to secure Thy triumph upon earth and to exalt Our Cause above all men, though no king be found who would turn his face towards Thee.

24    Call Thou to remembrance Thine arrival in the City, how the Ministers of the Sultán thought Thee to be unacquaint-ed with their laws and regulations, and believed Thee to be one of the ignorant. Say: Yea, by My Lord! I am ignorant of all things except what God hath, through His bountiful favor, been pleased to teach Me. To this We assuredly testify, and unhesitatingly confess it.

25    Say: If the laws and regulations to which ye cleave be of your own making, We will, in no wise, follow them. Thus have I been instructed by Him Who is the All-Wise, the All-Informed. Such hath been My way in the past, and such will it remain in the future, through the power of God and His might. This, indeed, is the true and right way. If they be ordained by God, bring forth, then, your proofs, if ye be of them that speak the truth. Say: We have written down in a Book which leaveth not unrecorded the work of any man, however insignificant, all that they have imputed to Thee, and all that they have done unto Thee.

26    Say: It behooveth you, O Ministers of State, to keep the precepts of God, and to forsake your own laws and regu-lations, and to be of them who are guided aright. Better is this for you than all ye possess, did ye but know it. If ye transgress the commandment of God, not one jot or one

tittle of all your works shall be acceptable in His sight. Ye shall, erelong, discover the consequences of that which ye shall have done in this vain life, and shall be repaid for them. This, verily, is the truth, the undoubted truth.

How great the number of those who, in bygone ages, have 27 committed the things ye have committed, and who, though superior to you in rank, have, in the end, returned unto dust, and been consigned to their inevitable doom! Would that ye might ponder the Cause of God in your hearts! Ye shall follow in their wake, and shall be made to enter a habitation wherein none shall be found to befriend or help you. Ye shall, of a truth, be asked of your doings, shall be called to account for your failure in duty with regard to the Cause of God, and for having disdainfully rejected His loved ones who, with manifest sincerity, have come unto you.

It is ye who have taken counsel together regarding them, 28 ye that have preferred to follow the promptings of your own desires, and forsaken the commandment of God, the Help in Peril, the Almighty.

Say: What! Cleave ye to your own devices, and cast 29 behind your backs the precepts of God? Ye, indeed, have wronged your own selves and others. Would that ye could perceive it! Say: If your rules and principles be founded on justice, why is it, then, that ye follow those which accord with your corrupt inclinations and reject such as conflict with your desires? By what right claim ye, then, to judge fairly between men? Are your rules and principles such as to justify your persecution of Him Who, at your bidding, hath presented Himself before you, your rejection of Him, and your infliction on Him every day of grievous injury? Hath

He ever, though it be for one short moment, disobeyed you? All the inhabitants of 'Iráq, and beyond them every discerning observer, will bear witness to the truth of My words.

30    Be fair in your judgment, O ye Ministers of State! What is it that We have committed that could justify Our banishment? What is the offense that hath warranted Our expulsion? It is We Who have sought you, and yet, behold how ye refused to receive Us! By God! This is a sore injustice that ye have perpetrated—an injustice with which no earthly injustice can measure. To this the Almighty is Himself a witness.

31    Have I at any time transgressed your laws, or disobeyed any of your ministers in 'Iráq? Inquire of them, that ye may act with discernment towards Us and be numbered with those who are well-informed. Hath anyone ever brought before them a plaint against Us? Hath anyone amongst them ever heard from Us a word contrary to that which God hath revealed in His Book? Bring forth, then, your evidence, that We may approve your actions and acknowledge your claims!

32    Had ye wished to deal with Us in accordance with your principles and standards, it would have behooved you to respect and honor Us for complying with your commands and following that which ye have pleased to ordain. Likewise, it would have beseemed you to repay the debts which We incurred in 'Iráq in the execution of your wishes. Ye should have given ear then unto Us, heard the account of Our woes, and judged with equity, as ye would judge your own selves. Ye should not have wished for Us that which ye have not wished for yourselves, but rather chosen to act with generosity. By God! Ye dealt with Us neither in accordance with your own principles and standards, nor with those of any man living, but in accordance with the promptings of

your evil and wayward passions, O ye concourse of the froward and the arrogant!

O Bird of Holiness! Soar in the heaven of communion with Me, and acquaint the people with that which We disclosed unto Thee in the billowing oceans of immortality beyond the mount of glory. Let the fear of no one dismay Thee, and put Thy trust in God, the Almighty, the Beneficent. We, verily, shall protect Thee from those who, without a clear token from God or an enlightening Book, have grievously wronged Thee. 33

Say: God is My witness, O concourse of the negligent! We came not unto you to spread disorder in your lands or to sow dissension amongst your peoples. Nay rather, We came in obedience to the command of the sovereign, and in order to exalt your authority, to instruct you in the ways of Our wisdom, and to remind you of that which ye had forgotten—even as He saith in truth: "Warn them, for, in truth, Thy warning will profit the believers."[70] But ye hearkened not unto the sweet melodies of the Spirit, and gave ear unwittingly unto Our enemies, they who follow the promptings of their corrupt inclinations, whose deeds the Evil One hath made fair-seeming in their own eyes, and whose tongues utter calumnies against Us. Heard ye not that which hath been revealed in His all-glorious and unerring Book: "If a wicked man come to you with news, clear it up at once"?[71] Wherefore have ye then cast the command of God behind your backs, and followed in the footsteps of them that are bent on mischief? 34

We have heard that one of these calumniators hath alleged that this Servant practiced usury whilst residing in 'Iráq, and was engaged in amassing riches for Himself. Say: How can 35 ye judge a matter whereof ye have no knowledge? How can ye hurl calumnies against the servants of God, and entertain such evil suspicions? And how could this accusation be true, when God hath forbidden this practice unto His servants in that most holy and well-guarded Book revealed unto Muḥammad, the Apostle of God and the Seal of the Prophets, a Book which He hath ordained to be His abiding testimony, and His guidance and monition unto all mankind? This is but one of the matters in which We have opposed the divines of Persia, inasmuch as We have, according to the text of the Book, forbidden unto all men the practice of usury. God Himself beareth witness to the truth of My words. "Yet I hold not myself clear, for the soul is prone to evil."[72] We intend only to impart unto you the truth, that ye might be informed thereof and be of them that lead a godly life. Beware lest ye give ear to the words of those from whom the foul smell of malice and envy can be discerned; pay no heed to them, and stand ye for righteousness.

36     Know ye that the world and its vanities and its embellishments shall pass away. Nothing will endure except God's Kingdom which pertaineth to none but Him, the Sovereign Lord of all, the Help in Peril, the All-Glorious, the Almighty. The days of your life shall roll away, and all the things with which ye are occupied and of which ye boast yourselves shall perish, and ye shall, most certainly, be summoned by a company of His angels to appear at the spot where the limbs of the entire creation shall be made to tremble, and the flesh of every oppressor to creep. Ye shall be asked of the things your hands have wrought in this, your vain life, and shall be repaid for your doings. This is the day that shall inevitably come upon you, the hour that none can put back. To this

the Tongue of Him that speaketh the truth and is the Knower of all things hath testified.

Fear God, ye inhabitants of the City, and sow not the     37
seeds of dissension amongst men. Walk not in the paths of
the Evil One. Walk ye, during the few remaining days of
your life, in the ways of the one true God. Your days shall
pass away as have the days of them who were before you. To
dust shall ye return, even as your fathers of old did return.

Know ye that I am afraid of none except God. In none but     38
Him have I placed My trust; to none will I cleave but Him,
and wish for naught except the thing He hath wished for
Me. This, indeed, is My heart's desire, did ye but know it. I
have offered up My soul and My body as a sacrifice for God,
the Lord of all worlds. Whoso hath known God shall know
none but Him, and he that feareth God shall be afraid of no
one except Him, though the powers of the whole earth rise
up and be arrayed against him. I speak naught except at His
bidding, and follow naught, through the power of God and
His might, except His truth. He, verily, shall recompense
the truthful.

Narrate, O Servant, the things Thou didst behold at the     39
time of Thine arrival in the City, that Thy testimony may
endure amongst men, and serve as a warning unto them that
believe. We found, upon Our arrival in the City, its gover-
nors and elders as children gathered about and disporting
themselves with clay. We perceived no one sufficiently mature to acquire from Us the truths which God hath taught
Us, nor ripe for Our wondrous words of wisdom. Our inner
eye wept sore over them, and over their transgressions and
their total disregard of the thing for which they were created.
This is what We observed in that city, and which We have

chosen to note down in Our Book, that it may serve as a warning unto them, and unto the rest of mankind.

40      Say: If ye be seekers after this life and the vanities thereof, ye should have sought them while ye were still enclosed in your mothers' wombs, for at that time ye were continually approaching them, could ye but perceive it. Ye have, on the other hand, ever since ye were born and attained maturity, been all the while receding from the world and drawing closer to dust. Why, then, exhibit such greed in amassing the treasures of the earth, when your days are numbered and your chance is well-nigh lost? Will ye not, then, O heedless ones, shake off your slumber?

41      Incline your ears to the counsels which this Servant giveth you for the sake of God. He, verily, asketh no recompense from you and is resigned to what God hath ordained for Him, and is entirely submissive to God's Will.

42      The days of your life are far spent, O people, and your end is fast approaching. Put away, therefore, the things ye have devised and to which ye cleave, and take firm hold on the precepts of God, that haply ye may attain that which He hath purposed for you, and be of them that pursue a right course. Delight not yourselves in the things of the world and its vain ornaments, neither set your hopes on them. Let your reliance be on the remembrance of God, the Most Exalted, the Most Great. He will, erelong, bring to naught all the things ye possess. Let Him be your fear, and forget not His covenant with you, and be not of them that are shut out as by a veil from Him.

43      Beware that ye swell not with pride before God, and disdainfully reject His loved ones. Defer ye humbly to the faithful, they that have believed in God and in His signs,

whose hearts witness to His unity, whose tongues proclaim His oneness, and who speak not except by His leave. Thus do We exhort you with justice, and warn you with truth, that perchance ye may be awakened.

Lay not on any soul a load which ye would not wish to 44 be laid upon you, and desire not for anyone the things ye would not desire for yourselves. This is My best counsel unto you, did ye but observe it.

Respect ye the divines and learned amongst you, they 45 whose conduct accords with their professions, who transgress not the bounds which God hath fixed, whose judgments are in conformity with His behests as revealed in His Book. Know ye that they are the lamps of guidance unto them that are in the heavens and on the earth. They who disregard and neglect the divines and learned that live amongst them—these have truly changed the favor with which God hath favored them.

Say: Wait ye till God will have changed His favor unto 46 you. Nothing whatsoever escapeth Him. He knoweth the secrets both of the heavens and of the earth. His knowledge embraceth all things. Rejoice not in what ye have done, or will do in the future, nor delight in the tribulation with which ye have afflicted Us, for ye are unable by such means as these to exalt your stations, were ye to examine your works with acute discernment. Neither will ye be capable of detracting from the loftiness of Our state. Nay, God will add unto the recompense with which He shall reward Us, for having sustained with persevering patience the tribulations We have suffered. He, verily, shall increase the reward of them that endure with patience.

Know ye that trials and tribulations have, from time im- 47 memorial, been the lot of the chosen Ones of God and His beloved, and such of His servants as are detached from all else but Him, they whom neither merchandise nor traffic beguile from the remembrance of the Almighty, they that speak not till He hath spoken, and act according to His commandment. Such is God's method carried into effect of old, and such will it remain in the future. Blessed are the steadfastly enduring, they that are patient under ills and hardships, who lament not over anything that befalleth them, and who tread the path of resignation.

48     That which hath befallen Us hath been witnessed before. Ours is not the first goblet dashed to the ground in the lands of Islám, nor is this the first time that such schemers have intrigued against the beloved of the Lord. The tribulations We have sustained are like unto the trials endured aforetime by Imám Ḥusayn. For he was approached by messengers from malicious and evil-hearted plotters, inviting him to come forth from the city; yet when he came unto them, accompanied by his kindred, they rose up against him with all their might, until at last they slew him, slaughtered his sons and his brothers, and took captive the remainder of his family. So did it come to pass in an earlier age, and God, verily, is a witness unto My words. Of his lineage there survived none, whether young or old, save his son 'Alí al-Awsat, known as Zaynu'l-'Ábidín.

49     Behold then, O heedless ones, how brightly the fire of the love of God blazed aforetime in the heart of Ḥusayn, if ye be of them that ponder! So intense grew its flame that fervor and longing at last seized the reins of patience from his grasp, and the love of Him Who is the All-Compelling so enraptured his heart that he surrendered his soul, his spirit, his substance, and his all in the path of God, the Lord

of the worlds. By God! Sweeter was this in his sight than the empire of earth and heaven. For the true lover desireth naught save reunion with his beloved and the seeker hath no goal but to attain unto the object of his quest. Their hearts long for reunion even as the body yearneth for the spirit, nay greater indeed is their longing, could ye but perceive it!

Say: That same fire now blazeth in Mine own breast, and My wish is that this Ḥusayn may lay down His life in like manner, in the hope of attaining unto so august and sublime a station, that station wherein the servant dieth to himself and liveth in God, the Almighty, the Exalted, the Great. Were I to disclose unto you the mysteries which God hath enshrined therein, ye would, of a truth, offer up your lives in His path, renounce your riches, and forsake all that ye possess, that ye might attain this transcendent and all-glorious station. God, however, hath veiled your hearts and obscured your eyes, lest ye should apprehend His mysteries and be made aware of their meaning. 50

Say: The sincere soul longeth for nearness to God even as the suckling babe yearneth for its mother's breast, nay more ardent is his longing, could ye but know it! Again, his long-ing is even as the panting of one sore athirst after the living waters of grace, or the yearning of the sinner for forgiveness and mercy. Thus do We expound unto you the mysteries of the Cause, and impart unto you what shall render you inde-pendent of all that hath so far occupied you, that perchance ye may enter the Court of Holiness within this exalted Par-adise. I swear by God! Whoso entereth therein shall never abandon its precincts, and whoso gazeth thereon shall never turn away therefrom, even should the swords of infidels and deniers rain blows upon him. Thus have We related unto 51 you that which befell Ḥusayn, and We beseech God that He may destine for Us that which He had decreed for him. He, verily, is the Most Generous, the All-Bountiful.

52    By the righteousness of God! Through his deed the fragrances of holiness were wafted over all things, the proof of God was perfected, and His testimony made manifest to all men. And after him God raised up a people who avenged his death, who slew his enemies, and who wept over him at dawn and at eventide. Say: God hath pledged in His Book to lay hold upon every oppressor for his tyranny, and to uproot the stirrers of mischief. Know ye that such holy deeds exert, in themselves, a great influence upon the world of being—an influence which is, however, inscrutable to all save those whose eyes have been opened by God, whose hearts He hath freed from obscuring veils, and whose souls He hath guided aright.

53    The day is approaching when God will have raised up a people who will call to remembrance Our days, who will tell the tale of Our trials, who will demand the restitution of Our rights from them that, without a tittle of evidence, have treated Us with manifest injustice. God, assuredly, dominateth the lives of them that wronged Us, and is well aware of their doings. He will, most certainly, lay hold on them for their sins. He, verily, is the fiercest of avengers.

54    Thus have We recounted unto you the tales of the one true God, and sent down unto you the things He had preordained, that haply ye may ask forgiveness of Him, may return unto Him, may truly repent, may realize your misdeeds, may shake off your slumber, may be roused from your heedlessness, may atone for the things that have escaped you, and be of them that do good. Let him who will, ac-

knowledge the truth of My words; and as to him that willeth not, let him turn aside. My sole duty is to remind you of your failure in duty towards the Cause of God, if perchance ye may be of them that heed My warning. Wherefore, hearken ye unto My speech, and return ye to God and repent, that He, through His grace, may have mercy upon you, may wash away your sins, and forgive your trespasses. The greatness of His mercy surpasseth the fury of His wrath, and His grace encompasseth all who have been called into being and been clothed with the robe of life, be they of the past or of the future.

O concourse of Ministers of State! Do ye believe in your 55 hearts that We have come to divest you of your earthly possessions and vanities? Nay, by the One in Whose hand is My soul! Our intention hath been to make clear that We oppose not the commands of the sovereign, nor are We to be numbered with the rebellious. Know ye of a certainty that all the treasures of the earth, all the gold, the silver, and the rare and precious gems they contain, are, in the sight of God, of His chosen ones and His loved ones, as worthless as a handful of clay. For erelong all that is on earth shall perish, and the kingdom will remain unto God, the All-Powerful, the Incomparable. That which perisheth can never profit Us, nor can it profit you, were ye but to reflect.

By the righteousness of God! I speak not falsely, and utter 56 naught save that which God hath bidden Me. To this bear witness the very words of this Tablet, if ye but reflect upon its contents. Follow not the promptings of your own desires, nor the whisperings of the Evil One in your souls. Follow rather the Cause of God, both in your outward and your inner lives, and be not of the heedless. Better is this for you than all that ye have laid up in your houses, and all that ye have sought by day and night.

57    The world will pass away, and so will all the things whereat your hearts rejoice, or wherein ye pride yourselves before men. Cleanse the mirrors of your hearts from the dross of the world and all that is therein, that they may reflect the resplendent light of God. This, indeed, shall enable you to dispense with all save God, and to attain unto the good pleasure of your Lord, the Most Bountiful, the All-Knowing, the All-Wise. We, verily, have unfolded before your eyes that which shall profit you both in this world and in the realm of faith, and which will lead you to the path of salvation. Would that ye might turn thereunto!

58    Hearken, O King,* to the speech of Him that speaketh the truth, Him that doth not ask thee to recompense Him with the things God hath chosen to bestow upon thee, Him Who unerringly treadeth the straight Path. He it is Who summoneth thee unto God, thy Lord, Who showeth thee the right course, the way that leadeth to true felicity, that haply thou mayest be of them with whom it shall be well.

59    Beware, O King, that thou gather not around thee such ministers as follow the desires of a corrupt inclination, as have cast behind their backs that which hath been committed into their hands and manifestly betrayed their trust. Be bounteous to others as God hath been bounteous to thee, and abandon not the interests of thy people to the mercy of such ministers as these. Lay not aside the fear of God, and be thou of them that act uprightly. Gather around thee those ministers from whom thou canst perceive the fragrance of

---

* Sulṭán ‘Abdu’l-‘Azíz.

faith and of justice, and take thou counsel with them, and choose whatever is best in thy sight, and be of them that act generously.

Know thou for a certainty that whoso disbelieveth in     60
God is neither trustworthy nor truthful. This, indeed, is the truth, the undoubted truth. He that acteth treacherously towards God will, also, act treacherously towards his king. Nothing whatever can deter such a man from evil, nothing can hinder him from betraying his neighbor, nothing can induce him to walk uprightly.

Take heed that thou resign not the reins of the affairs     61
of thy state into the hands of others, and repose not thy confidence in ministers unworthy of thy trust, and be not of them that live in heedlessness. Shun them whose hearts are turned away from thee, and place not thy confidence in them, and entrust them not with thine affairs and the affairs of such as profess thy faith. Beware that thou allow not the wolf to become the shepherd of God's flock, and surrender not the fate of His loved ones to the mercy of the malicious. Expect not that they who violate the ordinances of God will be trustworthy or sincere in the faith they profess. Avoid them, and preserve strict guard over thyself, lest their devices and mischief hurt thee. Turn away from them, and fix thy gaze upon God, thy Lord, the All-Glorious, the Most Bountiful. He that giveth up himself wholly to God, God shall, assuredly, be with him; and he that placeth his complete trust in God, God shall, verily, protect him from whatsoever may harm him, and shield him from the wickedness of every evil plotter.

Wert thou to incline thine ear unto My speech and ob-     62
serve My counsel, God would exalt thee to so eminent a

position that the designs of no man on the whole earth can ever touch or hurt thee. Observe, O King, with thine inmost heart and with thy whole being, the precepts of God, and walk not in the paths of the oppressor. Seize thou, and hold firmly within the grasp of thy might, the reins of the affairs of thy people, and examine in person whatever pertaineth unto them. Let nothing escape thee, for therein lieth the highest good.

63     Render thanks unto God for having chosen thee out of the whole world, and made thee king over them that profess thy faith. It well beseemeth thee to appreciate the wondrous favors with which God hath favored thee, and to magnify continually His name. Thou canst best praise Him if thou lovest His loved ones, and dost safeguard and protect His servants from the mischief of the treacherous, that none may any longer oppress them. Thou shouldst, moreover, arise to enforce the law of God amongst them, that thou mayest be of those who are firmly established in His law.

64     Shouldst thou cause rivers of justice to spread their waters amongst thy subjects, God would surely aid thee with the hosts of the unseen and of the seen, and would strengthen thee in thine affairs. No God is there but Him. All creation and its empire are His. Unto Him return the works of the faithful.

65     Place not thy reliance on thy treasures. Put thy whole confidence in the grace of God, thy Lord. Let Him be thy trust in whatever thou doest, and be of them that have submitted themselves to His Will. Let Him be thy helper and enrich thyself with His treasures, for with Him are the treasuries of the heavens and of the earth. He bestoweth them upon whom He will, and from whom He will He withholdeth

them. There is none other God but Him, the All-Possessing, the All-Praised. All are but paupers at the door of His mercy; all are helpless before the revelation of His sovereignty, and beseech His favors.

Overstep not the bounds of moderation, and deal justly 66 with them that serve thee. Bestow upon them according to their needs, and not to the extent that will enable them to lay up riches for themselves, to deck their persons, to embellish their homes, to acquire the things that are of no benefit unto them, and to be numbered with the extravagant. Deal with them with undeviating justice, so that none among them may either suffer want, or be pampered with luxuries. This is but manifest justice.

Allow not the abject to rule over and dominate them 67 who are noble and worthy of honor, and suffer not the high-minded to be at the mercy of the contemptible and worthless, for this is what We observed upon Our arrival in the City, and to it We bear witness. We found among its inhabitants some who were possessed of an affluent fortune and lived in the midst of excessive riches, while others were in dire want and abject poverty. This ill beseemeth thy sovereignty, and is unworthy of thy rank.

Let My counsel be acceptable to thee, and strive thou to 68 rule with equity among men, that God may exalt thy name and spread abroad the fame of thy justice in all the world. Beware lest thou aggrandize thy ministers at the expense of thy subjects. Fear the sighs of the poor and of the upright in heart who, at every break of day, bewail their plight, and be unto them a benignant sovereign. They, verily, are thy treasures on earth. It behooveth thee, therefore, to safeguard thy treasures from the assaults of them who wish to rob thee.

Inquire into their affairs, and ascertain, every year, nay every month, their condition, and be not of them that are careless of their duty.

69    Set before thine eyes God's unerring Balance and, as one standing in His Presence, weigh in that Balance thine actions every day, every moment of thy life. Bring thyself to account ere thou art summoned to a reckoning, on the Day when no man shall have strength to stand for fear of God, the Day when the hearts of the heedless ones shall be made to tremble.

70    It behooveth every king to be as bountiful as the sun, which fostereth the growth of all beings, and giveth to each its due, whose benefits are not inherent in itself, but are ordained by Him Who is the Most Powerful, the Almighty. The King should be as generous, as liberal in his mercy as the clouds, the outpourings of whose bounty are showered upon every land, by the behest of Him Who is the Supreme Ordainer, the All-Knowing.

71    Have a care not to entrust thine affairs of state entirely into another's hands. None can discharge thy functions better than thine own self. Thus do We make clear unto thee Our words of wisdom, and send down upon thee that which can enable thee to pass over from the left hand of oppression to the right hand of justice, and approach the resplendent ocean of His favors. Such is the path which the kings that were before thee have trodden, they that acted equitably towards their subjects, and walked in the ways of undeviating justice.

72    Thou art God's shadow on earth. Strive, therefore, to act in such a manner as befitteth so eminent, so august a station. If thou dost depart from following the things We have caused

to descend upon thee and taught thee, thou wilt, assuredly, be derogating from that great and priceless honor. Return, then, and cleave wholly unto God, and cleanse thine heart from the world and all its vanities, and suffer not the love of any stranger to enter and dwell therein. Not until thou dost purify thine heart from every trace of such love can the brightness of the light of God shed its radiance upon it, for to none hath God given more than one heart. This, verily, hath been decreed and written down in His ancient Book. And as the human heart, as fashioned by God, is one and undivided, it behooveth thee to take heed that its affections be, also, one and undivided. Cleave thou, therefore, with the whole affection of thine heart, unto His love, and withdraw it from the love of anyone besides Him, that He may aid thee to immerse thyself in the ocean of His unity, and enable thee to become a true upholder of His oneness. God is My witness. My sole purpose in revealing to thee these words is to sanctify thee from the transitory things of the earth, and aid thee to enter the realm of everlasting glory, that thou mayest, by the leave of God, be of them that abide and rule therein.

Hast thou heard, O King, what We have suffered at the 73 hands of thy ministers and how We have been treated by them, or art thou of the negligent? If indeed thou hast heard and known, wherefore didst thou not forbid thy ministers to commit such deeds? How didst thou desire for Him Who hath complied with thy command, and been obedient to thy behest, that which no king would desire for any of his subjects? And if thou knowest not, this indeed is a more grievous error, wert thou of the God-fearing. Wherefore shall I recount to thee that which We have suffered at the hands of these oppressors.

74    Know, then, that We came unto thy city at thine own behest, and entered therein with conspicuous honor. They expelled Us, however, from thy city with an abasement with which no abasement on earth can compare, if thou be of them that are well-informed. They made Us journey until We reached the place* which none entereth except such as have rebelled against the authority of the sovereign, and as are numbered with the transgressors. All this, notwithstanding that We had never disobeyed thee, though it be for a single moment, for when We heard thy bidding We observed it and submitted to thy will. In dealing with Us, however, thy ministers neither honored the standards of God and His commandments, nor heeded that which hath been revealed to the Prophets and Messengers. They showed Us no mercy and committed against Us that which no one among the faithful hath ever wrought against his fellow, nor any believer inflicted upon an infidel. God knoweth and is a witness unto the truth of Our words.

75    When they expelled Us from thy city, they placed Us in such conveyances as the people use to carry baggage and the like. Such was the treatment We received at their hands, shouldst thou wish to know the truth. Thus were We sent away, and thus were We brought to the city which they regard as the abode of rebels. Upon our arrival, We could find no house in which to dwell, and perforce resided in a place where none would enter save the most indigent stranger. There We lodged for a time, after which, suffering increasingly from the confined space, We sought and rented houses which by reason of the extreme cold had been vacated by

---

* Adrianople.

their occupants. Thus in the depth of winter we were con-
strained to make our abode in houses wherein none dwell
except in the heat of summer. Neither My family, nor those
who accompanied Me, had the necessary raiment to protect
them from the cold in that freezing weather.

Would that thy ministers had dealt with Us according 76
to the principles they uphold amongst themselves! For, by
God, they dealt with Us neither in accordance with the commandments of God, nor with the practices they uphold, nor
with the standards current amongst men, nor even with the
manner in which the destitute of the earth receive a wayfar-
er. Such is the account of what We suffered at their hands,
and which We have related unto thee in a language of truthfulness and sincerity.

All this befell Me, though I had come unto them at their 77
own behest and did not oppose their authority, which de-
riveth from thine own. Thus did We accept and observe
their bidding. They, however, appear to have forgotten that
which God hath commanded. He saith, and His Word is the
truth: "Act with humility towards the believers."[73] Methinks
that their only concern was their own comfort and repose,
and that their ears were deaf to the sighs of the poor and
the cries of the oppressed. They seem to imagine that they
have been created from pure light, while others have been
fashioned out of dust. How wretched are their imaginings!
We have all been created from a sorry germ.[74]

I swear by God, O King! It is not My wish to make My 78
plaint to thee against them that persecute Me. I only plead
My grief and My sorrow to God, Who hath created Me and
them, Who well knoweth our state and Who watcheth over
all things. My wish is to warn them of the consequences of

their actions, if perchance they might desist from treating others as they have treated Me, and be of them that heed My warning.

79 The tribulations that have touched Us, the destitution from which We suffer, the various troubles with which We are encompassed, shall all pass away, as shall pass away the pleasures in which they delight and the affluence they enjoy. This is the truth which no man on earth can reject. The days in which We have been compelled to dwell in the dust will soon be ended, as will the days in which they occupied the seats of honor. God shall, assuredly, judge with truth between Us and them, and He, verily, is the best of judges.

80 We render thanks unto God for whatsoever hath befallen Us, and We patiently endure the things He hath ordained in the past or will ordain in the future. In Him have I placed My trust; and into His hands have I committed My Cause. He will, certainly, repay all them that endure with patience and put their confidence in Him. His is the creation and its empire. He exalteth whom He will, and whom He will He doth abase. He shall not be asked of His doings. He, verily, is the All-Glorious, the Almighty.

81 Let thine ear be attentive, O King, to the words We have addressed to thee. Let the oppressor desist from his tyranny, and cut off the perpetrators of injustice from among them that profess thy faith. By the righteousness of God! The tribulations We have sustained are such that any pen that recounteth them cannot but be overwhelmed with anguish. No one of them that truly believe and uphold the unity of God can bear the burden of their recital. So great have been Our sufferings that even the eyes of Our enemies have wept over Us, and beyond them those of every discerning

person. And to all these trials have We been subjected, in spite of Our action in approaching thee, and in bidding the people to enter beneath thy shadow, that thou mightest be a stronghold unto them that believe in and uphold the unity of God.

Have I, O King, ever disobeyed thee? Have I, at any time, 82 transgressed any of thy laws? Can any of thy ministers that represented thee in 'Iráq produce any proof that can establish My disloyalty to thee? Nay, by Him Who is the Lord of all worlds! Not for one short moment did We rebel against thee, or against any of thy ministers. Never, God willing, shall We revolt against thee, though We be exposed to trials more severe than any We suffered in the past.

In the daytime and in the night season, at even and at 83 morn, We pray to God on thy behalf, that He may graciously aid thee to be obedient unto Him and to observe His commandment, that He may shield thee from the hosts of the evil ones. Do, therefore, as it pleaseth thee, and treat Us as befitteth thy station and beseemeth thy sovereignty. Be not forgetful of the law of God in whatever thou desirest to achieve, now or in the days to come. Say: Praise be to God, the Lord of all worlds!

Dost thou imagine, O Minister of the Sháh in the City, 84 that I hold within My grasp the ultimate destiny of the Cause of God? Thinkest thou that My imprisonment, or the shame I have been made to suffer, or even My death and utter annihilation, can deflect its course? Wretched is what thou hast imagined in thine heart! Thou art indeed of them that walk after the vain imaginings which their hearts devise. No God is there but Him. Powerful is He to manifest His Cause, and to exalt His testimony, and to establish whatsoever is His Will, and to elevate it to so eminent a position that neither thine own hands, nor the hands of them that have turned away from Him, can ever touch or harm it.

85      Dost thou believe thou hast the power to frustrate His Will, to hinder Him from executing His judgment, or to deter Him from exercising His sovereignty? Pretendest thou that aught in the heavens or in the earth can resist His Faith? Nay, by Him Who is the Eternal Truth! Nothing whatsoever in the whole of creation can thwart His Purpose. Cast away, therefore, the mere conceit thou dost follow, for mere conceit can never take the place of truth. Be thou of them that have truly repented and returned to God, the God Who hath created thee, Who hath nourished thee, and made thee a minister among them that profess thy faith.

86      Know thou, moreover, that He it is Who hath, by His own behest, created all that is in the heavens and all that is on the earth. How can, then, the thing that hath been created at His bidding prevail against Him? High is God exalted above what ye imagine about Him, ye people of malice! If this Cause be of God, no man can prevail against it; and if it be not of God, the divines amongst you, and they that follow their corrupt desires and such as have rebelled against Him will surely suffice to overpower it.

87      Hast thou not heard what a man of the family of Pharaoh, a believer, hath said of old, and which God recounted unto His Apostle, Whom He hath chosen above all human beings, and entrusted with His Message, and made the source of His mercy unto all them that dwell on earth? He said, and He, verily, speaketh the truth: "Will ye slay a man because he saith my Lord is God, when he hath already come to you with proofs of his mission? And if he be a liar, on him will

be his lie, but if he be a man of truth, part at least of what he threateneth will fall upon you."⁷⁵ This is what God hath revealed unto His Well-Beloved One, in His unerring Book.

And yet, ye have failed to incline your ears unto His bidding, have disregarded His law, have rejected His counsel as recorded in His Book, and have been of them that have strayed far from Him. How many those who, every year, and every month, have because of you been put to death! How manifold the injustices ye have perpetrated—injustices the like of which the eye of creation hath not seen, which no chronicler hath ever recorded! How numerous the babes and sucklings who were made orphans, and the fathers who lost their sons, because of your cruelty, O ye unjust doers! How oft hath a sister pined away and mourned over her brother, and how oft hath a wife lamented after her husband and sole sustainer!

Your iniquity waxed greater and greater until ye slew Him Who had never taken His eyes away from the face of God, the Most Exalted, the Most Great.* Would that ye had put Him to death after the manner men are wont to put one another to death! Ye slew Him, however, in such circumstances as no man hath ever witnessed. The heavens wept sore over Him, and the souls of them who are nigh unto God cried out for His affliction. Was He not a Scion of your Prophet's ancient House? Had not His fame as a direct descendant of the Apostle been spread abroad amongst you? Why, then, did ye inflict upon Him what no man, however far ye may look back, hath inflicted upon another? By God! The eye of

_____

* The Báb.

creation hath never beheld your like. Ye slay Him Who is a Scion of your Prophet's House, and rejoice and make merry while seated on your seats of honor! Ye utter your imprecations against them who were before you, and who have perpetrated what ye have perpetrated, and remain yourselves all the time unaware of your enormities!

90     Be fair in your judgment. Did they whom ye curse, upon whom ye invoke evil, act differently from yourselves? Have they not slain the descendant of their Prophet* as ye have slain the descendant of your own? Is not your conduct similar to their conduct? Wherefore, then, claim ye to be different from them, O ye sowers of dissension amongst men?

91     And when ye took away His life, one of His followers arose to avenge His death. He was unknown of men, and the design he had conceived was unnoticed by anyone. Eventually he committed what had been preordained. It behooveth you, therefore, to attach blame to no one except to yourselves, for the things ye have committed, if ye but judge fairly. Who is there on the whole earth who hath done what ye have done? None, by Him Who is the Lord of all worlds!

92     All the rulers and kings of the earth honor and revere the descendants of their Prophets and holy men, could ye but perceive it. Ye, on the other hand, are responsible for such acts as no man hath, at any time, performed. Your misdeeds have caused every understanding heart to be consumed with grief. And yet, ye have remained sunk in your heedlessness, and failed to realize the wickedness of your actions.

93     Ye have persisted in your waywardness until ye rose up against Us, though We had committed nothing to justify

---

* Imám Ḥusayn.

your enmity. Fear ye not God Who hath created you, and fashioned you, and caused you to attain your strength, and joined you with them that have resigned themselves to Him?* How long will ye persist in your waywardness? How long will ye refuse to reflect? How long ere ye shake off your slumber and are roused from your heedlessness? How long will ye remain unaware of the truth?

Ponder in thine heart. Did ye, notwithstanding your be- 94 havior and the things your hands have wrought, succeed in quenching the fire of God or in putting out the light of His Revelation—a light that hath enveloped with its brightness them that are immersed in the billowing oceans of immortality, and hath attracted the souls of such as truly believe in and uphold His unity? Know ye not that the Hand of God is over your hands, that His irrevocable Decree transcendeth all your devices, that He is supreme over His servants, that He is equal to His Purpose, that He doth what He wisheth, that He shall not be asked of whatever He willeth, that He ordaineth what He pleaseth, that He is the Most Powerful, the Almighty? If ye believe this to be the truth, wherefore, then, will ye not cease from troubling and be at peace with yourselves?

Ye perpetrate every day a fresh injustice, and treat Me as 95 ye treated Me in times past, though I never attempted to meddle with your affairs. At no time have I opposed you, neither have I rebelled against your laws. Behold how ye have, at the last, made Me a prisoner in this far-off land!

---

* The Muslims.

Know for a certainty, however, that whatever your hands or the hands of the infidels have wrought will never, as they never did of old, change the Cause of God or alter His ways.

96     Give heed to My warning, ye people of Persia! If I be slain at your hands, God will assuredly raise up one who will fill the seat made vacant through My death, for such is God's method carried into effect of old, and no change can ye find in God's method of dealing. Seek ye to put out God's light that shineth upon His earth? Averse is God from what ye desire. He shall perfect His light, albeit ye abhor it in the secret of your hearts.

97     Pause for but a little while and reflect, O Minister, and be fair in thy judgment. What is it that We have committed that could justify thee in having slandered Us unto the King's Ministers, in following thy desires, in perverting the truth, and in uttering thy calumnies against Us? We have never met each other except when We met thee in thy father's house, in the days when the martyrdom of Imám Ḥusayn was being commemorated. On those occasions no one could have had the chance of making known to others his views and beliefs in conversation or in discourse. Thou wilt bear witness to the truth of My words, if thou be of the truthful. I have frequented no other gatherings in which thou couldst have learned My mind or in which any other could have done so. How, then, didst thou pronounce thy verdict against Me, when thou hadst not heard My testimony from Mine own lips? Hast thou not heard what God, exalted be His glory, hath said: "Say not to everyone who meeteth you with a greeting, 'Thou art not a believer.'"[76] "Thrust not away those who cry to their Lord at morn and even, craving to behold His face."[77] Thou hast indeed forsaken what the

Book of God hath prescribed, and yet thou deemest thyself to be a believer!

Despite what thou hast done I entertain—and to this God is My witness—no ill will against thee, nor against anyone, though from thee and others We receive such hurt as no believer in the unity of God can sustain. My cause is in the hand of none except God, and My trust is in no one else but Him. Erelong shall your days pass away, as shall pass away the days of those who now, with flagrant pride, vaunt themselves over their neighbor. Soon shall ye be gathered together in the presence of God, and shall be asked of your doings, and shall be repaid for what your hands have wrought, and wretched is the abode of the wicked doers! 98

By God! Wert thou to realize what thou hast done, thou wouldst surely weep sore over thyself, and wouldst flee for refuge to God, and wouldst pine away and mourn all the days of thy life, till God will have forgiven thee, for He, verily, is the Most Generous, the All-Bountiful. Thou wilt, however, persist, till the hour of thy death, in thy heedlessness, inasmuch as thou hast, with all thine heart, thy soul and inmost being, busied thyself with the vanities of the world. Thou shalt, after thy departure, discover what We have revealed unto thee, and shalt find all thy doings recorded in the Book wherein the works of all them that dwell on earth, be they greater or less than the weight of an atom, are noted down. Heed, therefore, My counsel, and hearken thou, with the hearing of thine heart, unto My speech, and be not careless of My words, nor be of them that reject My truth. Glory not in the things that have been given thee. Set before thine eyes what hath been revealed in the Book of God, the Help in Peril, the All-Glorious: "And when they 99 had forgotten their warnings, We set open to them the gates of all things," even as We did set open to thee and to thy like the gates of this earth and the ornaments thereof. Wait thou, therefore, for what hath been promised in the latter part of this holy verse,[78] for this is a promise from Him Who is the Almighty, the All-Wise—a promise that will not prove untrue.

100    I know not the path ye have chosen and which ye tread, O congregation of My ill-wishers! We summon you to God, We remind you of His Day, We announce unto you tidings of your reunion with Him, We draw you nigh unto His court, and send down upon you tokens of His wondrous wisdom, and yet lo, behold how ye reject Us, how ye condemn Us, through the things which your lying mouths have uttered, as an infidel, how ye devise your devices against Us! And when We manifest unto you what God hath, through His bountiful favor, bestowed upon Us, ye say, "It is but plain magic." The same words were spoken by the generations that were before you and were what ye are, did ye but perceive it. Ye have thereby deprived yourselves of the bounty of God and of His grace, and shall never obtain them till the day when God will have judged between Us and you, and He, verily, is the best of judges.

101    Certain ones among you have said: "He it is Who hath laid claim to be God." By God! This is a gross calumny. I am but a servant of God Who hath believed in Him and in His signs, and in His Prophets and in His angels. My tongue, and My heart, and My inner and My outer being testify that there is no God but Him, that all others have been created by His behest, and been fashioned through the operation of His Will. There is none other God but Him, the Creator,

the Raiser from the dead, the Quickener, the Slayer. I am He that telleth abroad the favors with which God hath, through His bounty, favored Me. If this be My transgression, then I am truly the first of the transgressors. I and My kindred are at your mercy. Do ye as ye please, and be not of them that hesitate, that I might return to God My Lord, and reach the place where I can no longer behold your faces. This, indeed, is My dearest wish, My most ardent desire. Of My state God is, verily, sufficiently informed, observant.

Imagine thyself to be under the eye of God, O Minister! 102 If thou seest Him not, He, in truth, clearly seeth thee. Observe, and judge fairly Our Cause. What is it that We have committed that could have induced thee to rise up against Us, and to slander Us to the people, if thou be of them who are just? We departed out of Ṭihrán, at the bidding of the King,* and, by his leave, transferred Our residence to 'Iráq. If I had transgressed against him, why, then, did he release Me? And if I were innocent of guilt, wherefore did ye afflict Us with such tribulation as none among them that profess your faith hath suffered? Hath any of Mine acts, after Mine arrival in 'Iráq, been such as to subvert the authority of the government? Who is it that can be said to have detected anything reprehensible in Our behavior? Inquire for thyself of its people, that thou mayest be of them who have discerned the truth.

For eleven years We dwelt in that land, until the Min- 103 ister representing thy government arrived,[79] whose name Our pen is loath to mention, who was given to wine, who

---

* Náṣiri'd-Dín Sháh.

followed his lusts, and committed wickedness, and was corrupt and corrupted ʻIráq. To this will bear witness most of the inhabitants of Baghdád, wert thou to inquire of them, and be of such as seek the truth. He it was who wrongfully seized the substance of his fellow-men, who forsook all the commandments of God, and perpetrated whatever God had forbidden. Eventually, he, following his desires, rose up against Us, and walked in the ways of the unjust. He accused Us, in his letter to thee, and thou didst believe him and followed in his way, without seeking any proof or trustworthy evidence from him. Thou didst ask for no explanation, nor didst thou attempt either to investigate or ascertain the matter, that the truth might be distinguished from falsehood in thy sight, and that thou mightest be clear in thy discernment. Find out for thyself the sort of man he was by asking those Ministers who were, at that time, in ʻIráq, as well as the Governor of the City* and its high Counselor, that the truth may be revealed to thee, and that thou mayest be of the well-informed.

104     God is Our witness! We have, under no circumstances, opposed either him, or others. We observed, under all conditions, the precepts of God, and were never one of those that wrought disorders. To this he himself doth testify. His intention was to lay hold on Us, and send Us back to Persia, that he might thereby exalt his fame and reputation. Thou hast committed the same crime, and for the selfsame purpose. Ye both are of equal grade in the sight of God, the sovereign Lord of all, the All-Knowing.

---

* Baghdád.

It is not Our purpose in addressing to thee these words to 105
lighten the burden of Our woe, or to induce thee to inter-
cede for Us with anyone. Nay, by Him Who is the Lord of
all worlds! We have set forth the whole matter before thee,
that perchance thou might realize what thou hast done,
might desist from inflicting on others the hurt thou hast inflicted on Us, and might be of them that have truly repented
to God, Who created thee and created all things, and might
act with discernment in the future. Better is this for thee
than all thou dost possess, than thy ministry whose days are
numbered.

Beware lest thou be led to connive at injustice. Set thy 106
heart firmly upon justice, and alter not the Cause of God,
and be of them whose eyes are directed towards the things
that have been revealed in His Book. Follow not, under any
condition, the promptings of thine evil desires. Keep thou
the law of God, thy Lord, the Beneficent, the Ancient of
Days. Thou shalt most certainly return to dust, and shalt
perish like all the things in which thou takest delight. This is
what the Tongue of truth and glory hath spoken.

Rememberest thou not God's warning uttered in times 107
past, that thou mayest be of them that heed His warning?
He said, and He, verily, speaketh the truth: "From it (earth)
have We created you, and unto it will We return you, and
out of it will We bring you forth a second time."[80] This is
what God ordained unto all them that dwell on earth, be
they high or low. It behooveth not, therefore, him who was
created from dust, who will return unto it, and will again be
brought forth out of it, to swell with pride before God, and
before His loved ones, to proudly scorn them, and be filled
with disdainful arrogance. Nay, rather it behooveth thee and

those like thee to submit yourselves to them Who are the Manifestations of the unity of God, and to defer humbly to the faithful, who have forsaken their all for the sake of God, and have detached themselves from the things which engross men's attention, and lead them astray from the path of God, the All-Glorious, the All-Praised. Thus do We send down upon you that which shall profit you and profit them that have placed their whole trust and confidence in their Lord.

108    O ye divines of the City! We came to you with the truth, whilst ye were heedless of it. Methinks ye are as dead, wrapt in the coverings of your own selves. Ye sought not Our presence, when so to do would have been better for you than all your doings. Know ye that the Sun of vicegerency hath dawned in all truth, and yet ye have turned away therefrom. The Moon of guidance hath risen high in the midmost heaven, and yet ye remain veiled therefrom. The Star of divine bounty hath shone forth above the horizon of eternal holiness, and yet ye have strayed far therefrom.

109    Know ye, that had your leaders, to whom ye owe allegiance, and on whom ye pride yourselves, and whom ye mention by day and by night, and from whose traces ye seek guidance—had they lived in these days, they would have circled around Me, and would not have separated themselves from Me, whether at eventide or at morn. Ye, however, did not turn your faces towards My face, for even less than a moment, and waxed proud, and were careless of this Wronged One, Who hath been so afflicted by men that they dealt with Him as they pleased. Ye failed to inquire about My condition, nor did ye inform yourselves of the things which befell Me. Thereby have ye withheld from yourselves

the winds of holiness, and the breezes of bounty, that blow from this luminous and perspicuous Spot.

Methinks ye have clung to outward things, and forgotten   110 the inner things, and say that which ye do not. Ye are lovers of names, and appear to have given yourselves up to them. For this reason make ye mention of the names of your leaders. And should anyone like them, or superior unto them, come unto you, ye would flee him. Through their names ye have exalted yourselves, and have secured your positions, and live and prosper. And were your leaders to reappear, ye would not renounce your leadership, nor would ye turn in their direction, nor set your faces towards them.

We found you, as We found most men, worshipping   111 names which they mention during the days of their life, and with which they occupy themselves. No sooner do the Bearers of these names appear, however, than they repudiate them, and turn upon their heels. Thus have We found you, and thus have We reckoned up your actions and borne witness to all your doings in this day. Know ye that God will not, in this day, accept your thoughts, nor your remembrance of Him, nor your turning towards Him, nor your devotions, nor your vigilance, unless ye be made new in the estimation of this Servant, could ye but perceive it.

By God! The Tree of vicegerency hath been planted, the   112 Point of knowledge hath been made plain, and the sovereignty of God, the Help in Peril, the Self-Subsisting, hath been established. Fear ye the Lord. Follow not the promptings of your evil desires, but keep the law of God all your days. Renew the rules of the ways ye follow, that ye may be led by the light of guidance and may hasten in the path of the True One.

113    O ye wise men of the City and philosophers of the world! Beware lest human learning and wisdom cause you to wax proud before God, the Help in Peril, the Self-Subsisting. Know ye that true wisdom is to fear God, to know Him, and to recognize His Manifestations. This wisdom, however, can be attained only by those who detach themselves from the world, and who walk in the ways of the good pleasure of their Lord. Are ye possessed of greater wisdom than the one who contrived a moon which would rise from one well and set in another, and whose light was visible at a distance of three leagues?[81] God, verily, blotted out every trace of his works and returned him unto dust, as ye have already heard or are now informed.

114    How many the sages and philosophers who equaled or surpassed him in learning and wisdom! And how vast the number of those who equaled or surpassed yourselves! Some of them believed in God, while others disbelieved and joined partners with Him. The latter were at last cast into the Fire, there to take up their abode, while the former returned unto the mercy of their Lord, therein to abide. For God doth not ask you of your sciences, but of your faith and of your conduct. Are ye greater in wisdom than the One Who brought you into being, Who fashioned the heavens and all that they contain, the earth and all that dwell upon it? Gracious God! True wisdom is His. All creation and its empire are His. He bestoweth His wisdom upon whomsoever He chooseth amongst men, and withholdeth it from whomsoever He desireth. He, in truth, is the Bestower and the Withholder, and He, verily, is the All-Bountiful, the All-Wise.

115    O ye learned of the world! Ye failed to seek Our presence, that ye might hearken unto the sweet melodies of the Spirit

and perceive that which God in His bounty hath pleased to bestow upon Me. Verily, this grace hath now escaped you, did ye but know. Had ye sought Our presence, We would have imparted unto you a knowledge that would have rendered you independent of all else. But this ye failed to do, and thus hath the decree of God been fulfilled. Now have I been forbidden to disclose it, since We stand accused of sorcery, if ye perceive Our meaning. The same words were uttered by the deniers of old, men whom death hath long since overtaken and who now dwell in the fire bewailing their plight. The deniers of this day shall likewise meet their doom. Such is the irrevocable decree of Him Who is the All-Powerful, the Self-Sufficient.

I counsel you, in the end, not to overstep the bounds of God, nor to heed the ways and habits of men, for these can neither "fatten nor appease your hunger." Fix, rather, your gaze upon the precepts of God. Whosoever desireth, let him accept this counsel as a path leading unto his Lord, and whosoever desireth, let him return to his own idle imaginings. My Lord, verily, is independent above all who are in the heavens and on the earth, and above all that they say and do. 116

I close with these words uttered by God, exalted be His glory: "Say not to everyone who meeteth you with a greeting, 'Thou art not a believer.'"[82] 117

Peace be upon you, O concourse of the faithful, and praise be to God, the Lord of the worlds. 118

# ENDNOTES

1. cf. Qur'án 2:30–34; 38:71–75.

2. Ustád Muḥammad-'Alíy-i-Salmání. See *God Passes By*, pp. 166–168, for an account of the events referred to by Bahá'u'lláh in this and following paragraphs.

3. The word *Haykal* (Temple) is composed in Arabic of the four letters *Há', Yá', Káf* and *Lám* (HYKL). Its first letter is taken to symbolize the word *Huvíyyah* (Essence of Divinity); its second letter the word *Qadír* (Almighty), of which *Yá'* is the third letter; its third letter the word *Karím* (All-Bountiful); and its fourth letter the word *Faḍl* (Grace), of which Lám is the third letter.

4. cf. Qur'án 21:30; 24:45; 25:54.

5. That is, the letter "E." In all such instances in the Writings where the letters "B" and "E" are mentioned, the Arabic letters are *Káf* and *Nún*, the two consonants of the Arabic word *Kun*, which is the imperative meaning "Be."

6. "The tree beyond which there is no passing," a reference to the station of the Manifestation of God.

7. These are examples of the types of questions put to the Báb. According to the teachings of Shí'ite Islám, leadership of the Islamic community belonged of right, after

the passing of the Prophet Muḥammad, to a line of twelve successors, descendants of His daughter Fáṭimih, known as "Imáms." This line being eventually severed through the "occultation" of the last Imám, communication with the latter was for a time maintained through a succession of four intermediaries known as "Gates."

8. One of a trio of Arabian goddesses whose worship was abolished by the Prophet Muḥammad.

9. A small rock situated low in the eastern corner of the Kaaba.

10. cf. Matthew 5:29; Mark 9:47.

11. This is Bahá'u'lláh's second Tablet addressed to the French Emperor. An earlier Tablet was revealed in Adrianople.

12. The Crimean War (1853–1856).

13. Within the year Napoleon III was defeated at the Battle of Sedan (1870) and sent into exile.

14. cf. Qur'án 77:20; 32:8.

15. The two Most Great Festivals are the Festival of Riḍván, during which Bahá'u'lláh first proclaimed His Mission, and the Declaration of the Báb. The "twin days" refer to the Birthdays of the Báb and Bahá'u'lláh. cf. Kitáb-i-Aqdas, ¶110.

16. cf. Qur'án 17:78.

17. Mírzá Buzurg Khán, the Persian Consul-General in Baghdád.

18. The Mu'taminu'l-Mulk, Mírzá Sa'íd Khán-i-Anṣárí, Minister of Foreign Affairs.

19. Bahá'u'lláh here refers to His and His companions' application for Ottoman citizenship.

20. Áqá Siyyid Muḥammad-i-Ṭabáṭabá'íy-i-Isfáhání, known as "Mujáhid."

21. The second Russo-Persian War of 1825–28.

22. Qur'án 2:94; 62:6.

23. cf. Persian Hidden Words, nos. 24, 25, 28 and 30.

24. Qur'án 49:6.

25. Qur'án 5:59.

26. A Tradition ascribed to the eleventh Imám, Abú Muḥammad al-Ḥasan al-'Askarí.

27. Traditions ascribed to the sixth Imám, Abú 'Abdu'lláh Ja'far aṣ-Ṣádiq.

28. Shaykh Murtaḍáy-i-Anṣárí, a prominent mujtahid.

29. Qur'án 2:179.

30. Qur'án 6:164; 17:15; 35:18; 39:7; 53:38.

31. cf. Qur'án 3:40; 14:27; 22:18.

32. cf. Qur'án 5:1.

33. cf. Qur'án 5:64.

34. Qur'án 40:5.

35. Qur'án 36:30.

36. Qur'án 8:30.

37. Qur'án 6:35.

38. cf. Matthew 24:35; Mark 13:31; Luke 21:33.

39. John 14:28.

40. cf. John 14:16; 14:26; 15:26; 16:7.

41. See, for example, Qur'án 4:46; 5:13; 5:41; and 2:75, and the discussion in the Kitáb-i-Íqán, p. 84 ff.

42. 'Alí Ibn Ḥusayn, known as "Zaynu'l-'Ábidín," the second of the Imám Ḥusayn's sons, who became the fourth Imám.

43. The Khárijites, a faction opposed to both the Imáms and the Umayyad state.

44. Allusions to the 'Abbásid and Umayyad dynasties, respectively.

45. Qur'án 57:16.

46. cf. Luke 19:21.

47. cf. Qur'án 55:26.

48. cf. Qur'án 12:31.

49. This Tablet was revealed in Arabic in honor of Ḥájí Muḥammad Ismá'íl-i-Káshání, entitled <u>Dh</u>abíḥ (Sacrifice) and Anís (Companion) by Bahá'u'lláh, and addresses 'Alí Páshá, the Ottoman Prime Minister, referred to here as Ra'ís (Chief or Ruler).

50. Sulṭán 'Abdu'l-'Azíz lost both his throne and his life in 1876. During the subsequent war with Russia (1877–1878), Adrianople was occupied by the enemy and the Turks experienced a violent bloodbath.

51. Literally, "the Mount of Figs" and "the Mount of Olives," Cf. Qur'án 95:1.

52. Chosroes II, the Sasanian monarch who reigned in Persia during the lifetime of Muḥammad.

53. Ḥájí Ja'far-i-Tabrízí; he was prevented in time from ending his life.

54. Siyyid Ismá'íl of Zavárih.

55. This second Tablet of Bahá'u'lláh addressing 'Alí Páshá was revealed in Persian shortly after Bahá'u'lláh's arrival and confinement in 'Akká.

56. For an account of this incident see Shoghi Effendi, *God Passes By* (Wilmette, IL: Bahá'í Publishing Trust, 1974), p. 182.

57. A probable reference to the fire of Hocapaṣa, which destroyed a large part of the city of Constantinople in 1865.

58. The Lawḥ-i-Fu'ád was addressed to <u>Sh</u>aykh Káẓim-i-Samandar of Qazvín, one of the apostles of Bahá'u'lláh. Its subject, the former Ottoman statesman Fu'ád Páshá, died in

France in 1869. The letter names Káf and Ẓá refer to the K and Ẓ of Kázim.

59. Cf. Qur'án 38:3.

60. Cf. Qur'án 13:13.

61. Cf. Qur'án 40:32.

62. Cf. Qur'án 38:12, 89:10.

63. "heart" translates *fu'ád*, the given name of the Ottoman minister.

64. Mírzá Mihdíy-i-Rashtí, a judge in Constantinople and supporter of Mírzá Yaḥyá.

65. John 14:28.

66. John 16:13.

67. John 1:13.

68. The French Ambassador in Constantinople.

69. The Persian Ambassador in Constantinople.

70. Qur'án 51:55.

71. Qur'án 49:6.

72. Qur'án 12:53.

73. Qur'án 15:88.

74. Cf. Qur'án 77:20; 32:8.

75. Qur'án 40:28.

76. Qur'án 4:94.

77. Qur'án 6:52.

78. Qur'án 6:44.

79. The Persian Consul-General in Baghdád.

80. Qur'án 20:55.

81. Al-Muqanna' of Khurásán (eighth century A.D.).

82. Qur'án 4:94.

# GLOSSARY

**'Abdu'l-Ghaffár.** One of several companions of Bahá'u'lláh who were condemned to exile on the island of Cyprus. In despair over his separation from Bahá'u'lláh, he threw himself into the sea but was rescued, resuscitated, and forced to continue his journey to Cyprus. After two years there, he managed to escape and rejoin Bahá'u'lláh in 'Akká.

**Abraham.** Considered by Bahá'ís to be a Prophet, or Manifestation of God, He is also recognized as the founder of monotheism and the father of the Jewish and Arab peoples. Muḥammad, the Báb, and Bahá'u'lláh are among His descendants.

**Adrianople.** Present-day Edirne, a city in European Turkey to which Bahá'u'lláh and His family were exiled in 1863, and where they resided for five years.

**'Akká (Acre).** A four-thousand-year-old seaport located on the coast of present-day Israel. In the mid-nineteenth century 'Akká was a penal colony of the Ottoman Empire. In 1868 Bahá'u'lláh and His family and companions were banished there by Sulṭán 'Abdu'l-'Azíz. Because of the privations suffered within its walls Bahá'u'lláh named 'Akká "the Most Great Prison."

**'Alí al-Awsat.** See Zaynu'l-'Ábidín.

**'Alí Páshá.** (1815–71) Ottoman prime minister who was partially responsible for Bahá'u'lláh's banishment to the prison-city of 'Akká.

**Ancient Beauty,** A translation of *Jamál-i-Qadím,* a name of God that is also used as a title of Bahá'u'lláh, Whom Bahá'ís believe to be the latest Manifestation of God to humankind. One cannot always say categorically in any passage whether the reference is to God, to Bahá'u'lláh, or to both.

**Annas.** High priest of the Jews and father-in-law to Caiaphas (see John 18:13).

**Anís.** Literally *Close Companion.* Surname of Muḥammad-'Alíy-i-Zunúzí, the youth who was martyred with the Báb in 1850.

**Báb, the.** Literally *the Gate:* title assumed by Siyyid 'Alí-Muḥammad (20 October 1819–9 July 1850) after declaring His mission in 1844. The Báb's station is twofold: He is a Manifestation of God and Founder of the Bábí Faith, and He is the Herald of Bahá'u'lláh.

**Báb, Declaration of the.** The anniversary commemorating the Báb's declaration of His prophetic mission to His first disciple, Mullá Ḥusayn, on 23 May 1844 in S͟híráz.

**Bábí.** Follower of the Báb.

**Badíʻ.** (c. 1852–69) Literally *unique, wonderful:* title given by Bahá'u'lláh to the seventeen-year-old youth who delivered Bahá'u'lláh's Tablet to Náṣiri'd-Dín S͟háh. Bahá'u'lláh praised his heroism and gave him the title "Pride of Martyrs."

**Bahá, people of.** Followers of Bahá'u'lláh; Bahá'ís.

**Bahá'í.** Of or pertaining to Bahá'u'lláh, used especially to denote His followers.

**Bahá'u'lláh.** *The Glory of God:* title of Mírzá Ḥusayn-'Alí (1817–1892), Prophet-Founder of the Bahá'í Faith. Bahá'ís refer to Him with a variety of titles, including the Promised One of All Ages, the Blessed Beauty, the Blessed Perfection, the Ancient Beauty. Bahá'ís consider His writings to be direct revelation from God.

**Baṭḥá.** Refers to Mecca; Baṭḥá is the central quarter and the lowest part of Mecca and lies in the immediate vicinity of the Ka'bih (Kaaba), Islam's most sacred shrine.

**Bayán.** *Exposition, explanation, lucidity, eloquence, utterance:* the title given by the Báb to two of His major works, one in Persian, the other in Arabic. It is also used sometimes to denote the entire body of His writings.

**Black Pit.** The subterranean dungeon of Ṭihrán in which Bahá'u'lláh was imprisoned August–December 1852 and in which He received the first intimations of His divine mission.

**Caiaphas.** The Jewish high priest who presided at the court that tried and condemned Jesus.

**Christ.** (c. 6–4 B.C.–A.D. 30) Recognized by Bahá'ís as a Manifestation of God and the founder of Christianity. The Bahá'í writings often refer to Christ as "the Spirit of God" and "the Son."

**Concourse on high.** The company of holy souls of the spiritual world.

**Constantinople.** Present-day Istanbul, Turkey.

**Covenant.** A pact that involves obligations by both parties. According to Bahá'u'lláh, God has promised to always guide and instruct humanity through a succession of Divine Messengers, Whom humanity has the obligation to accept and obey.

**Divine Lote-Tree.** A reference to the tree beyond which there is no passing—in ancient times, the tree that Arabs planted to mark the end of a road. In Islám the term symbolizes the point in the heavens beyond which neither humans nor angels can pass in their approach to God, thus delimiting the bounds of divine knowledge as revealed to humankind. In Bahá'í usage, it is a reference to the Manifestation of God—i.e., Bahá'u'lláh.

**Fáṭimih.** The daughter of Muḥammad. She married 'Alí, the cousin of Muḥammad, and had three sons. One died in infancy and the other two, Ḥasan and Ḥusayn, are considered by Sh͟í'ites to be the Second and Third Imáms, respectively.

**Fu'ád Pá͟shá.** (1815–69) Ottoman statesman who is the subject of the Lawḥ-i-Fu'ád.

**Ḥijáz (Hejaz).** A region in northwest present-day Saudi Arabia that is perhaps best known for the Islámic holy city of Mecca, which lies within it.

**Imám.** Designates in its most general sense an Islámic religious leader who leads the prayers in the mosque and, more particularly in Sh͟í'ih Islám, the twelve hereditary successors of the Prophet Muḥammad.

**Imám Ḥusayn.** (626–80) In Sh͟í'ih Islám, the Third Imám, son of 'Alí and Faṭimih and grandson of the Prophet Muḥammad. He was martyred at Karbilá, Iraq, in 680 A.D.

**Islám.** Literally *Submission to the Will of God:* The religion of Muḥammad, upheld by Bahá'ís as divine in origin.

**Jesus.** See Christ.

**Kaaba.** Literally *Cube:* The cube-like building in the courtyard of the great Mosque at Mecca that is the goal of Islámic pilgrimage and the point toward which Muslims turn in prayer.

**King of Islám.** An allusion to Sulṭán 'Abdu'l-'Azíz, reigning monarch of the Ottoman Empire from 1861 to 1876.

**Kitáb-i-Aqdas, the.** Literally *The Most Holy Book:* the chief repository of Bahá'u'lláh's laws and the Mother Book of His revelation.

**Land of Mystery.** An allusion to Adrianople, today known as Edirne, Turkey.

**Lawḥ-i-Fu'ád.** Tablet of Bahá'u'lláh whose subject is the former Ottoman statesman Fu'ád Páshá, who died in France in 1869. The tablet was addressed to one of Bahá'u'lláh's followers.

**Lawḥ-i-Sulṭán.** Tablet of Bahá'u'lláh addressed to Náṣiri'd-Dín Sháh.

**Manifestation of God.** Designation of a Prophet Who is the Founder of a religious Dispensation, inasmuch as in His words, His person, and His actions He manifests the nature and purpose of God in accordance with the capacity and needs of the people to whom He comes.

**Manifestation of His Cause.** See Manifestation of God.

**Manifestation(s).** See Manifestation of God.

**Mecca.** A city in Saudi Arabia that is the holy city of Islám and the birthplace of Muḥammad (A.D. 570). It is the principal place of pilgrimage for Muslims.

**Messenger of God.** Term used in the Bahá'í writings to refer to a Prophet, or Manifestation of God.

**Mírzá Yaḥyá.** (c. 1831/2–1912) A younger half-brother of Bahá'u'lláh who turned against Him and tried to kill Him. He later claimed to be the Báb's successor but was unsuccessful in his ambitions and was eventually exiled by the Ottoman government to Cyprus.

**Moses.** (circa 1300 b.c.) Founder of Judaism, regarded by Bahá'ís as a Manifestation of God.

**Mosque of Aqṣá.** The largest mosque in Jerusalem.

**Most Great Name.** The name Bahá'u'lláh (meaning in Arabic "the Glory of God") and its derivatives, such as *Alláh-u-Abhá* ("God is Most Glorious"), *Bahá* ("Glory," "Splendor," or "Light"), and *Yá Bahá'u'l-Abhá* ("O Thou the Glory of the Most Glorious!").

**Most Great Prison.** The walled prison-city of 'Akká (Acre) in which Bahá'u'lláh, His family, and a number of companions were confined from 31 August 1868 until June 1877.

**Muḥammad.** (A.D. 570–632) Prophet and Founder of Islám. Bahá'ís regard Muḥammad as a Manifestation of God and His book, the Qur'án, as holy scripture.

**Muḥammad Sháh.** (1807–48) Sháh, or king, of Persia from 1834–48 who imprisoned the Báb.

**Náṣiri'd-Dín Sháh.** (1831–96) Ruler of Persia during the time of Bahá'u'lláh. During his reign the Báb and thousands of His followers were executed.

**Nimrod.** A descendant of Ham represented in Genesis as a mighty hunter and a king of Shinar. According to Jewish and Islámic traditions, he persecuted Abraham and his name became symbolic of great pride.

**People of Bahá.** See Bahá, people of.

**People of the Bayán.** Followers of the Báb—Forerunner and Herald of Bahá'u'lláh—Whose greatest doctrinal work was the Bayán.

**Prophet.** See Manifestation of God.

**Riḍván, Festival of.** Riḍván is the Islámic name of the gardener and custodian of Paradise. In Bahá'í terminology the word denotes both "garden" and "paradise"; however, it has also ben used to denote God's good-pleasure and His divine acceptance. The Riḍván Festival, the holiest and most significant of all Bahá'í festivals, commemorates Bahá'u'lláh's declaration of His mission to His companions in the Garden of Riḍván in Baghdád in 1863. It is a twelve-day period celebrated annually 21 April–2 May.

**Saná'í.** A leading Persian mystic poet of the twelfth century.

**Shí'ih Islám.** One of the two major branches of Islám, the other being Sunní. Its followers view the descendants of 'Alí, son-in-law of the Prophet Muḥammad, as the only rightful successors to Muḥammad.

**Shoghi Effendi.** The title by which Shoghi Rabbání (1897–1957), great-grandson of Bahá'u'lláh, is known to Bahá'ís. He was appointed Guardian of the Bahá'í Faith and authorized interpreter of Bahá'u'lláh's writings.

**Sulṭán 'Abdu'l-'Azíz.** (1830–76) Ruler of the Ottoman Empire during whose reign Bahá'u'lláh and His family were forced to endure successive banishments.

**Sunní Islám.** Branch of Islám that accepts the authority of leaders known as caliphs and rejects the claims of the hereditary imáms.

**Súriy-i-Haykal.** Bahá'u'lláh's compilation of His summons addressed to the individual potentates of the world during His lifetime—Pope Pius IX, Napoleon III, Czar Alexander II, Queen Victoria, and Náṣiri'd-Dín Sháh.

**Súriy-i-Mulúk.** Literally *Súrih of Kings:* tablet revealed by Bahá'u'lláh in Adrianople to the kings of the world collectively. In it He boldly proclaims His station as Manifestation of God.

**Súriy-i-Ra'ís.** Tablet revealed by Bahá'u'lláh and addressed to 'Álí Páshá, the Ottoman prime minister during the time of Bahá'u'lláh.

**Tablet.** A term for a sacred epistle containing a revelation from God. The giving of the Law to Moses on tables, or tablets, is mentioned in Qur'án 7:142: "We wrote for him (Moses) upon tables *(alwah,* pl. of *lauh)* a monition concerning every matter." In Bahá'í scripture the term refers to letters revealed by Bahá'u'lláh and the Báb.

**Universal House of Justice.** The supreme governing and legislative body of the Bahá'í Faith.

**Zaynu'l-'Ábidín.** (658–712/3) In S͟hí'ih Islám, the fourth Imám and son of Imám Ḥusayn.

# NOTE ON THE TRANSLATION

Wherever possible, translations made by Shoghi Effendi have been incorporated in the present volume. These passages account for approximately one third of the text. The committees and individuals appointed to prepare the translations faced the challenge of rendering the balance of the Text in a manner at once faithful to the meaning of the original and consistent with the exalted English style established by the Guardian for the translation of Bahá'u'lláh's matchless utterance.

In the translation of the Lawḥ-i-Sulṭán the translators benefited from consulting the earlier, pioneering translation of the English orientalist E. G. Browne as it appeared in 'Abdu'l-Bahá's A Traveller's Narrative, first published by Cambridge University Press in 1891.

# KEY TO PASSAGES TRANSLATED
# BY SHOGHI EFFENDI

## Abbreviation of Sources

### ESW

Bahá'u'lláh. *Epistle to the Son of the Wolf.*
Wilmette: Bahá'í Publishing Trust, 1988.

### GPB

Shoghi Effendi. *God Passes By.*
Wilmette: Bahá'í Publishing Trust, 1974.

### GWB

Bahá'u'lláh. *Gleanings from the Writings of Bahá'u'lláh.*
Wilmette: Bahá'í Publishing, 2005.

### KI

Bahá'u'lláh. *The Kitáb-i-Íqán.*
Wilmette: Bahá'í Publishing, 2003.

# HW

Bahá'u'lláh. *The Hidden Words.*
Wilmette: Bahá'í Publishing, 2003.
(PHW are from the Persian Hidden Words.)

# PDC

Shoghi Effendi. *The Promised Day Is Come.*
Wilmette: Bahá'í Publishing Trust, 1996.

# WOB

Shoghi Effendi. *The World Order of Bahá'u'lláh: Selected Letters.*
Wilmette: Bahá'í Publishing Trust, 1991.

## SÚRIY-I-HAYKAL

| PARAGRAPH | PASSAGE | SOURCE |
|---|---|---|
| 6–7 | "While engulfed in tribulations . . . of them that perceive." | GPB 101–102 |
| 8 | "The day is approaching when God . . . the Self-Subsisting." | WOB 109–110 |
| 34 | "Erelong shall God draw forth . . . how vehement is His might" | WOB 110 |
| 42 | "Beware lest ye shed the blood . . . if ye do but understand." | ESW 25 |
| 44 | "Naught is seen in My temple . . . could be seen but God." | WOB 109 |
| 47 | "the fertilizing winds . . . whether seen or unseen!" | WOB 169, PDC ¶112 |
| 50 | "The Holy Spirit Itself . . . of them that comprehend" | WOB 109 |
| 66 | "Within the treasury of Our Wisdom . . . the All-Wise." | WOB 109 |
| 75 | "It is in Our power, should We wish it, to enable . . . future ages." | WOB 107 |

| PARAGRAPH | PASSAGE | SOURCE |
|---|---|---|
| 88 | "Great is the blessedness . . . the Almighty, the All-Wise." | PDC ¶271 |
| 89 | "O ye the dawning-places . . . and unto others." | PDC ¶208 |
| 89 | "Ye are even as a spring . . . it fruits, will be corrupted." | PDC ¶208 |
| 96 | "Had the Primal Point . . . with each other in My Days." | WOB 138 |

## POPE PIUS IX (Lawḥ-i-Páp)

| PARAGRAPH | PASSAGE | SOURCE |
|---|---|---|
| 102 | "O Pope! . . . the Almighty, the Unrestrained." | PDC ¶71 |
| 102 | "He, verily, hath again come . . . hath been illumined." | PDC ¶71 |
| 103 | "Dwellest thou in palaces . . . to-wards the Kingdom." | PDC ¶71 |
| 105 | "Arise in the name of thy Lord ... peoples of all faiths." | PDC ¶71 |
| 106 | "Call thou to remembrance . . . away from His light." | PDC ¶72 |
| 108 | "Consider those who opposed . . . disputed with Him." | PDC ¶72 |
| 108 | "None save a very few . . . even-tide and at dawn." | PDC ¶72 |
| 109 | "Read ye the Evangel . . . con-course of learned men!" | PDC ¶256 |
| 111 | "The fragrances of the . . . fast hold of guidance." | PDC ¶256 |
| 112 | "The Word which the Son . . . of the righteous!" | PDC ¶73 |
| 113 | "This is the day . . . Kingdom is fulfillled!" | PDC ¶73 |
| 114 | "My body longeth . . . from its transgressions." | PDC ¶73 |

| PARAGRAPH | PASSAGE | SOURCE |
|---|---|---|
| 115 | "The people of the Qur'án . . . clouds wept over Us." | PDC ¶247 |
| 116 | "And if they cast . . . the Gracious, the All-Powerful!" | WOB 108 |
| 118 | "O Supreme Pontiff . . . the book of creation." | PDC ¶74 |
| 120 | "Should the inebriation . . . Revealer of all power." | PDC ¶74 |
| 126 | "Verily, the day of ingathering . . . the All-Compelling." | PDC ¶74 |
| 127 | "Say: O concourse of Christians . . . turn ye unto Him." | PDC ¶261 |
| 127 | "The Beloved One . . . heedless of My Revelation" | PDC ¶261 |
| 128 | "O people of the Gospel! . . . everlasting life." | PDC ¶261 |
| 129 | "We behold you . . . Direct yourselves towards Him." | PDC ¶261 |
| 129 | "Verily, He said . . . quickeners of mankind." | PDC ¶261 |

## NAPOLEON III (Lawḥ-i-Napulyún II)

| PARAGRAPH | PASSAGE | SOURCE |
|---|---|---|
| 131–5 | "O King of Paris! . . . near access to God to flow." | ESW 46–49, GPB 207 |
| 136–9 | "Say: O concourse of monks . . . wrapt in a thick veil!" | ESW 49–52 |
| 140 | "More grievous . . . kingdoms of earth and heaven." | ESW 52 |
| 141 | "Upon Our arrival . . . token of God's grace." | GPB 206 |
| 142–43 | "As My tribulations multiplied . . . poor and the desolate." | ESW 52–53 |
| 143 | "Abandon thy palaces . . . them that turn unto Him." | PDC ¶70 |

| PARAGRAPH | PASSAGE | SOURCE |
|---|---|---|
| 143 | "Shouldst thou desire . . . All-Knowing, the All-Wise." | PDC ¶70 |
| 144 | "Arise thou . . . Lord of strength and of might." | ESW 53 |
| 145 | "Adorn the body . . . peoples of the earth." | ESW 53–54 |
| 146 | "Doth it behoove you . . . shining and resplendent Seat." | ESW 54 |
| 147 | "Shed not the blood . . . abode of the transgressors!" | ESW 54 |
| 148 | "God hath prescribed . . . influence his hearers." | GWB 158.1 |
| 149 | "Deal not treacherously . . . the Most Generous." | ESW 54–55 |
| 150–51 | "O people of Bahá . . . created of a sorry germ." | ESW 55 |
| 152 | "Regard ye the world . . . such as create dissension." | ESW 55–56 |
| 154 | "He Who is your Lord . . . among God's blessed ones." | GWB 107.1 |
| 156 | "Meditate on the world . . . this sublime Vision." | ESW 56 |

## CZAR ALEXANDER II (Lawḥ-i-Malik-i-Rús)

| PARAGRAPH | PASSAGE | SOURCE |
|---|---|---|
| 158 | "O Czar of Russia . . . barter away this sublime station." | PDC ¶75 |
| 159–60 | "Beware lest thy sovereignty . . . sword of the oppressor." | PDC ¶75–76 |
| 162–3 | "Again I say . . . the Mighty, the Glorified." | PDC ¶77–78 |
| 164 | "Some lamented . . . Evangel were adorned." | PDC ¶78 |
| 170 | "Blessed be the king . . . the All-Powerful, the Almighty." | PDC ¶78 |

## QUEEN VICTORIA (Lawḥ-i-Malikih)

| PARAGRAPH | PASSAGE | SOURCE |
|---|---|---|
| 171–3 | "O Queen in London . . . the Ruler, the All-Wise." | PDC ¶79–81 |
| 173 | "And if any one of them . . . of the blissful." | ESW 61–62 |
| 174–6 | "O ye the elected . . . all else naught but error." | GWB 120.1–3 |
| 176–7 | "Each time that Most Mighty . . . what I say." | ESW 63–64 |
| 178–82 | "O ye rulers . . . naught but manifest justice." | GWB 119.1–5 |
| 185 | "Turn thou unto God . . . heavens and of the earth." | PDC ¶82 |

## NÁSIRI'D-DÍN SHÁH (Lawḥ-i-Sulṭán)

| PARAGRAPH | PASSAGE | SOURCE |
|---|---|---|
| 192–95 | "O King! I was but a man . . . derived from the Name of God!" | PDC ¶97–99 |
| 217 | "A just king is the shadow . . . that hath surpassed the worlds." | PDC ¶182 |
| 221 | "Would that the world-adorning wish . . . for Me or against Me." | PDC ¶110 |
| 225 | "O ye that are foolish . . . the paths of perdition." | PHW #24 as quoted in ESW 15 |
| 226 | "O ye seeming fair . . . immeasurable is the difference!" | PHW #25 as quoted in ESW 16 |
| 227 | "O essence of desire! . . . unto the hosts of holiness." | PHW #28 |
| 228 | "O bondslave of the world! . . . returned whence it came." | PHW #30 |
| 230 | "O King of the age! . . . a sufficient witness unto Me." | PDC ¶100 |

| PARAGRAPH | PASSAGE | SOURCE |
|---|---|---|
| 231 | "The religious doctors . . . and unto them shall it return." | KI ¶275 |
| 233 | "When the Standard of Truth . . . shall curse it." | KI ¶267 |
| 234 | "Those doctors who have indeed drunk of the cup of renunciation" | GPB 143 |
| 242 | "Each nation hath plotted darkly . . . invalidate the truth." | KI ¶4 |
| 242 | "No Messenger cometh unto them but they laugh Him to scorn." | KI ¶4 |
| 244 | "But if their opposition be grievous . . . a ladder into heaven" | KI ¶116 |
| 249 | "O would that thou wouldst . . . knowledge of the Book." | PDC ¶101 |
| 249 | "But for the repudiation . . . no God is there but He!" | PDC ¶101 |
| 258 | "By Him Who is the Truth! . . . lighteth earth and heaven." | ESW 17 |
| 265 | "I have seen, O Sháh . . . nor ear heard." | PDC ¶102 |
| 265–6 | "How numerous the tribulations . . . in the path of My Lord!" | PDC ¶102 |
| 267 | "According to what they say . . . metropolis of the owl" | GPB 186 |
| 268 | "By God! Though weariness . . . such as commune with Him." | PDC ¶102 |
| 273 | "But for the tribulations . . . the Lord of the worlds." | ESW 94 |
| 276 | "Thus have We built the Temple . . . Be and it is." | PDC ¶113 |

# SÚRIY-I-RA'ÍS

| PARAGRAPH | PASSAGE | SOURCE |
|---|---|---|
| 1 | "Hearken, O chief . . . the Help in Peril, the Self-Subsisting." | WOB 178 |
| 2 | "Thou hast, O Chief, committed that . . . manifest loss!" | WOB 178, GPB 174 |
| 5 | "The day is approaching . . . in sore distress." | PDC ¶152 |
| 11 | "the loved ones of God . . . on the first night without food." | GPB 179 |
| 12 | "The people surrounded the house . . . wept over Us" | GPB 179 |
| 12 | "We perceived that the weeping . . . such as ponder." | GPB 179–180 |
| 13 | "unheard of in bygone centuries . . . the power of His might" | GPB 180 |
| 13 | "King and Beloved of Martyrs" | GPB 136–137 |
| 14 | "Say: This Youth hath departed . . . the power of truth" | GPB 181 |
| 18 | "Had Muḥammad . . . Thy law!" | WOB 105 |
|  | "Had Moses . . . Thy face!" | WOB 105–106 |
| 21 | "Ere long will God . . . the Almighty, the Beneficent" | PDC ¶185 |

# LAWḤ-I-RA'ÍS

| PARAGRAPH | PASSAGE | SOURCE |
|---|---|---|
| 6 | "From the foundation of the world . . . nor heard of." | GPB 187 |
| 7 | "Soon will He seize you . . . none to help or succor you." | PDC ¶153 |
| 9 | "Several times calamities . . . the Pen of My command." | PDC ¶153 |
| 25–26 | "There is a matter . . . may be made known unto you." | PDC ¶111 |

# LAWḤ-I-FU'ÁD

| PARAGRAPH | PASSAGE | SOURCE |
|---|---|---|
| 13 | "Soon will We dismiss . . . the All-Compelling." | PDC ¶156 |

# SÚRIY-I-MULÚK

| PARAGRAPH | PASSAGE | SOURCE |
|---|---|---|
| 2 | "O kings of the earth! . . . the All-Powerful, the All-Wise." | PDC ¶41 |
| 2–3 | "Fear God, O concourse . . . and be not of the heedless." | PDC ¶41 |
| 4 | "My face hath come forth . . . could ye but know it." | PDC ¶41 |
| 6 | "Arise, then, . . . may be revealed unto you." | PDC ¶41 |
| 6 | "Beware lest ye hinder . . . can be quickened." | PDC ¶41 |
| 7–14 | "Lay not aside the fear . . . the right course." | PDC ¶42–46 |
| 15 | "O kings of Christendom! . . . the entire creation." | PDC ¶64 |
| 20–23 | "Twenty years have passed . . . turn his face towards Thee." | GWB 116.2–5 |
| 24–30 | "Call Thou to remembrance . . . Himself a witness." | GWB 65.1–7 |
| 36 | "Know ye that the world . . . all things hath testified." | GWB 65.8 |
| 37–47 | "Fear God, ye inhabitants . . . the path of resignation." | GWB 66.1–11 |
| 53–54 | "The day is approaching . . . of the past or of the future." | GWB 66.12–13 |
| 58–72 | "Hearken, O King . . . abide and rule therein." | GWB 114.1–15 |
| 74 | "They expelled Us . . . on earth can compare" | GPB 161 |

| PARAGRAPH | PASSAGE | SOURCE |
|---|---|---|
| 74 | "the place which none entereth . . . authority of the sovereign" | GPB 161 |
| 75 | "Neither My family . . . that freezing weather." | GPB 161 |
| 78–83 | "I swear by God, O King! . . . the Lord of all worlds!" | GWB 114.16–21 |
| 84–107 | "Dost thou imagine . . . trust and confidence in their Lord." | GWB 113.1–24 |
| 108 | "O ye divines of the City! . . . than all your doings." | PDC ¶224 |
| 109–111 | "Know ye, that had your leaders . . . turn upon their heels." | PDC ¶224 |
| 111 | "Know ye that God will not . . . could ye but perceive it." | PDC ¶224 |

# INDEX

The references in the index refer to the individual Tablet, followed by the paragraph numbers within that Tablet. For example, a topic mentioned in the second paragraph of the Súriy-i-Mulúk is cited as M2. Within each entry and sub-entry the index references are arranged in the order that the Tablets appear in this book.

*Key to abbreviations:*

SÚRIY-I-HAYKAL ........................................................ H
SÚRIY-I-RA'IS ........................................................... SR
LAWḤ-I- RA'IS ............................................................ LR
LAWḤ-I-FU'ÁD ............................................................ F
SÚRIY-I-MULÚK ........................................................ M

'Abdu'l-'Azíz (Sulṭán of Turkey), H139, 183; F13, M58–83
    Bahá'u'lláh proposes meeting with, LR25–26
    mistreatment of Bahá'u'lláh, M73
    will lose Adrianople, SR5
'Abdu'l-Ghaffár, LR5
'Abdu'lláh-i-Ubayy, H243
Abraham, SR7, 18

Bahá'u'lláh made no request of, H216
banish Bahá'u'lláh, H267
bear dominion to aid God's Cause, H143
benign, M68
burden of expenditures laid on subjects, H179; M9
Christian, M15–16
creation entrusted to, H210
deeds of, M46
enforce the law of God, M63
establish peace, H178
of Ethiopia, H198
expenditures of, H179; M8
failure of, M15, 54
follow own desires (corrupt inclinations), M28–29
generosity (bounty) of, M70
honor descendants of their Prophets, M92
hypocrisy of, M89
insufficient that they listen to claimant alone, H229
just, H217, 259
manifestations of God's power, H210
ministers of, H158; LR12, 15; M17–18, 24, 26, 30, 31,
        55, 59, 61, 68, 73–74, 76, 82, 97, 102, 103
mistreated Bahá'u'lláh, M73
mortality of, H261, 269–70; LR19; M15, 36, 79, 98,
        106–7
must be equitable, H118
must be just, M9–13, 21, 66, 68
must establish peace, M8
must investigate matters, M103
must obey God's
        commandments, H118; M7, 12–14, 21, 26, 62

attempt on life of, H188; M91
Bahá'u'lláh loves for his own sake, H194
Bahá'u'lláh prays for, H238, 274
to be just to the Bahá'ís, H230
courtiers of, H194, 235
desire what God desires, H215
exiled Bahá'u'lláh, M102
freed Bahá'u'lláh from prison, M102
God's mercy to, H188
heart between God's fingers, H193
informed of misbehavior of his officials, H207
to keep God's commandments, H205
King of the Age, H206, 221, 230, 232
must decide for or against Bahá'u'lláh, H221
persecuted Bahá'ís, H220
raised up by faith and deeds, H199
received no account of Bahá'u'lláh's condition, H206
    to recognize Bahá'u'lláh, H195
shadow of God (sign of His power), H194
should aid the Bahá'í Faith, H275
should call meeting of Bahá'u'lláh and the divines, H221
should exercise justice, H190, 215
should exercise mercy, H215
sovereignty a contemptible possession, H195
station, if he believes, H195
treat subjects justly, H274
Nation(s), H112, 134, 242, 254
  Lord (Creator) of, H152, 268
  summoned to God, H160
Nimrod, SR7; F11

power of, H21, 150; SR17
praise of God, H21, 23, 134, 216
sword of, H42, 150, 212
teaching the Cause through, H150; SR20
*see also* Word(s)
Spirit, H60, 177, 227, 261; LR19; F12; M3, 115
of Bahá'u'lláh, H116, 162
body yearns for, M49
of God, H62
Holy, H50, 115, 133–34, 150; F16
human life proceeds from, SR33
Most Great, H50
same as soul, mind, sight, hearing, SR35
*see also* Jesus Christ
*see also* Soul(s)
Steadfastness, H27, 61, 155; SR41; F1, 13; M6, 14, 47
Strife (conflict; contention; dissension; hostility; etc.), H53,
147, 152, 188, 207–8, 213; LR17–18; M8, 34,
37, 90
forbidden as a means of rendering assistance unto God,
H210–14
Suffering, *see* Bahá'u'lláh, suffering of; Bahá'ís, suffering of
Suicide, SR13; LR5
Supplication, *see* Prayer
Syria, H171

Tablet(s), H31, 33, 43, 92, 96, 110, 129, 141, 155, 173, 182,
184, 202; SR26, 36, 38; LR24; M1, 6, 12, 56
Guarded, H158
lucid, H189
of Muḥammad, SR6

PUBLISHING

# BAHÁ'Í PUBLISHING
# AND THE BAHÁ'Í FAITH

Bahá'í Publishing produces books based on the teachings of the Bahá'í
Faith. Founded over 160 years ago, the Bahá'í Faith has spread to some
235 nations and territories and is now accepted by more than five million
people. The word "Bahá'í" means "follower of Bahá'u'lláh." Bahá'u'lláh,
the founder of the Bahá'í Faith, asserted that He is the Messenger of
God for all of humanity in this day. The cornerstone of His teachings
is the establishment of the spiritual unity of humankind, which will
be achieved by personal transformation and the application of clearly
identified spiritual principles. Bahá'ís also believe that there is but one
religion and that all the Messengers of God—among them Abraham,
Zoroaster, Moses, Krishna, Buddha, Jesus, and Muhammad—have
progressively revealed its nature. Together, the world's great religions are
expressions of a single, unfolding divine plan. Human beings, not God's
Messengers, are the source of religious divisions, prejudices, and hatreds.

The Bahá'í Faith is not a sect or denomination of another religion, nor is
it a cult or a social movement. Rather, it is a globally recognized independent
world religion founded on new books of scripture revealed by Bahá'u'lláh.

Bahá'í Publishing is an imprint of the National Spiritual Assembly of
the Bahá'ís of the United States.